34.95

LORRAINE FARRELLY

bar and restaurant

interior structures

WILEY-ACADEMY

For Martin, Tom & Ellen

Published in Great Britain in 2003 by Wiley-Academy,
a division of John Wiley & Sons Ltd

Copyright © 2003

John Wiley & Sons Ltd,
The Atrium, Southern Gate, Chichester,
West Sussex PO19 8SQ, England
Telephone (+44) 1243 779777
Email (for orders and customer service enquiries):
cs-books@wiley.co.uk
Visit our Home Page on:
www.wileyeurope.com or www.wiley.com

This publication is designed to provide accurate
and authoritative information in regard to the subject
matter covered. It is sold on the understanding
that the Publisher is not engaged in rendering
professional services. If professional advice or
other expert assistance is required, the services
of a competent professional should be sought.

Other Wiley Editorial Offices
John Wiley & Sons Inc., 111 River Street,
Hoboken, NJ 07030, USA
Jossey-Bass, 989 Market Street,
San Francisco, CA 94103-1741, USA
Wiley-VCH Verlag GmbH, Boschstr. 12,
D-69469 Weinheim, Germany
John Wiley & Sons Australia Ltd,
33 Park Road, Milton,
Queensland 4064, Australia
John Wiley & Sons (Asia) Pte Ltd,
2 Clementi Loop #02-01,
Jin Xing Distripark, Singapore 129809
John Wiley & Sons Canada Ltd,
22 Worcester Road, Etobicoke,
Ontario, Canada M9W 1L1

Wiley also publishes its books in a variety of
electronic formats. Some content that appears
in print may not be available in electronic books.

ISBN 0-471-48953-0

Set in Interstate
Designed by Neil Pereira
Printed and bound in Italy

contents

INTRODUCTION

The new millennium has heralded an explosion in the style and taste of interior spaces, perhaps nowhere more evident than in the interiors of bars and restaurants. Synonymous with reinterpretations of culture, the variety of restaurants and bars reflects the social, cultural and economic shifts that the last century has witnessed. The global movement of people and communities, precipitated by migration and war, plus the increased mobility afforded by more accessible air travel, has triggered new approaches to food, to drinking and eating which in turn have stimulated an unprecedented level of innovative responses in architecture and interior design.

In order to approach such a broad subject, and one which inevitably affects us all, I have divided the text into a series of investigations. First, I examine the idea of eating and drinking as social events and outline how the bar and restaurant have developed from the idea of the early coaching inns of medieval

England and Europe to evolve into the diverse range of restaurants and bars available today. Second, I consider the changes in culture that have affected the place of eating and drinking in the 20th century, a period in which travel and broader cultural ideas have meant that we have more interesting palates, that we no longer associate the notion of a particular food with a particular place as we would have at the end of the 19th century, when place and food were so specifically linked. Food and drink have become part of the global market, as have all commodities. Nor is what we eat any longer restricted by seasonal availability – strawberries can be transported from one hemisphere to the other in mid winter. Potatoes are as readily available from Egypt as from England; variations are beginning to lose their distinction.

Intimately connected to this new accessibility of international food and culture is the idea of how these new spaces are experienced, the concept of the hyper real. What are we experiencing when we go out to a bar and restaurant? Is it a form of virtual transportation to some architect or designer's imagined place, or an in-between place that is inspired by food, by its tastes and sensory experience to create a simulation of a reality? Add to this our feelings about genetically modified foods and the reality of tastes and the food itself become a construct. There is a need to return to the 'real', the organic. After over a century of relentless industrialisation of farming and production techniques there is a need to return to the organic past – to recapture the tastes, textures and smells of food pre-fertiliser, pre-industrialisation of crops and pre-intensive farming; we are interested in the idea of taste, 'real' taste.

    A restaurant which serves Asian/South American cuisine such as Asia de Cuba by Philippe Starck requires a transcontinental imagination in terms of creating flavours and an experience of place. Does such a hybrid exist? Perhaps anything is possible. The architectural components can be mixed as easily as the spices and ingredients of the restaurant to produce an exciting, unexpected melange; the setting can be as challenging in sensory and experiential terms as the meal itself.

The fourth part of the text considers the 'flexible interior'. Then of course there is the reality of the architectural space, that which exemplifies 21st-century architecture: flexible, indeterminate spaces. A bar one day, a restaurant the next. The interior space is a theme park, an unpredictable yet exciting experience in a fantastical place. The designer has to be one step ahead; to transport you from the everyday reality and predictability of life in the city to a place where anything is possible and dreams can become a reality.

Finally, the idea of 'globalisation' of food and drink concludes the introduction.

PART 1

Eating and drinking are two basic requirements for existence. The environment in which we undertake these activities can be purely functional; a simple refectory as a place for eating, or incredibly theatrical: a large banqueting hall with a table set for a hundred guests. The analogy of the restaurant to a theatre is appropriate. It is a function based activity, cooking, which is carried out in a sanitised, controlled environment, back stage; then there is the area where the diners sit, the platform for entertainment, the arena, where the product is beautifully and carefully presented in a pleasant environment and one much less functional and more formal in terms both of its layout and of the social codes which control it.

The contrast between the two environments, the kitchen as the 'servant' space and the 'served' spaces of the dining rooms, has dictated and controlled the response to the design and consideration of those spaces. This relates back to the hierarchical social structure which existed in the Georgian period and dictated the arrangement of space in a Georgian house. The servant spaces such as kitchen and bathroom were hidden; the 'served' spaces, dining room and sitting room, were celebrated areas, large and theatrical in terms of space and decoration.

It is an indication of affluent society that something functional has become an event. It is the notion of abundance of food and wealth that has created a society where to eat out is a common occurrence.

In the 21st century eating out has become something of a focus in western society. In some cultures dining out at a restaurant is part of everyday experience; in others it is socially separated, reserved for special occasions.

Eating in a restaurant may be a celebration or mark an event, clinch a deal or provide the appropriate ambience to discuss a business proposal. So the meal as event has a whole series of scenarios attached to it, each requiring a different set or scene, to determine and complement the

atmosphere or mood. The social context has encouraged the theatrical approach to the design of the restaurant interior; it determines a difference of flavour between restaurants. Le Cirque 2000 in New York by Adam Tihany International uses the analogy of the circus. The performance is the reference for the design of the space, offering a tantalising possibility of escape from the reality of the city.

The mood of the interior and the type of food served will create an attitude and attract a particular clientele. The type of person each venue attracts is determined by the price level of the menu and the particular atmosphere created, conditions which establish the restaurant's individuality and connection to a particular social group. All of this is influenced by location. To enter certain restaurants is to identify yourself with a particular world or attitude.

Historically, bars differ from restaurants. The evolution of the bar is different, somehow more colloquial. Bars or inns in the 18th century were linked to the notion of travel, and coaching inns providing beer and food – sustenance for the journey – owed their location to specific frequented routes. In cities, the bar or pub was the local place of entertainment, where gossip and rumour were exchanged over a pint; little has changed over the intervening centuries. Then beer and ale were local brews identifying people with place; now beer is as much a commodity as Coca-Cola, ubiquitously available, customers identifying with brand and label as much as place. To be seen in the right bar is as important as being seen in the right restaurant; it identifies a social and cultural group. The experience of being in a bar is more transitory than that of being in a restaurant, a connection back to the custom of bars providing refreshment en route.

The idea of the bar and restaurant as integral to popular culture is clear from their strong association with literature and cinema. *The Cook, the Thief, his Wife and her Lover*, directed by

THE HISTORY OF EATING AND DRINKING

Peter Greenaway, is on one level simply a film about characters and the lustful and unspeakable things they do to one another. It clearly illustrates the difference between the 'service' and 'served' areas of a restaurant whose function dictates the interior design: the set is constructed as though the building has been cut in section and the track shot across all of these different rooms as someone moves through the restaurant, exposing the connection between these separate spaces. It also demonstrates the connection of the restaurant experience with the idea of theatre and performance. The arrangement of the restaurant in terms of the preparation rooms of the kitchen and the clean, formal dining space reinforces this analogy. However, this customary separation is being challenged by the design of restaurant spaces where the preparation of food becomes the performance itself. Here the chef is located centre-stage, visibly chopping food and transforming ingredients through sleight of hand into mouth watering dishes. The chef is the cabaret. Perhaps it shatters the illusion of the mysterious preparation; or does it, rather, reveal the mechanics of the restaurant?

On another level, there is no end to the ideas stirred up by this pornographic imagery. Or is the film simply about a cook, a thief, his wife and her lover?

The thief's thuggish personality dominates the film and browbeats the others into submission. He is loud, large, criminal. Every night he presides over an obscene banquet in a London restaurant, where the other customers exhibit remarkable patience at his hog-like behaviour. He surrounds himself with cronies, hit-men, hangers-on, and with his long-suffering wife, for whom martyrdom has become a lifestyle.

At another table in the restaurant sits the lover, a book propped up so that he can read while he eats, one night his eyes meet the eyes of the thief's wife. Lightning strikes, and within seconds they are making passionate love in the ladies' room. The sex scenes are hungry and passionate and yet they are upstaged by the rest of the film, which is so uncompromising in its savagery that the sex seems tranquil by comparison.

Night after night the charade goes on – the thief acting monstrously, the cook enduring humiliation, the wife and her lover meeting to make love in the toilet, the kitchen, the meat room, the refrigerator, anywhere that is sufficiently inappropriate and uncomfortable. Greenaway gives a nightmare tinge to these scenes by using a different colour scheme for every locale – red for the dining room, white for the toilets – and by having the colour of the characters' costumes change as they walk from one to another. These colours and the idea of a chameleon, that the actor changes according to the scenario, are reminiscent of the experience the diner has in a contemporary restaurant: to become one with the interior space. The dining room is the stage for the main action.

The Cook, the Thief, his Wife and her Lover is more of a meditation on modern times in general. It is about the greed of an entrepreneurial class that distracts itself with romance and escapism. An apposite satire of the experience on offer in a contemporary restaurant: romance and escapism.

The Cook, the Thief, his Wife and her Lover is not an easy film to sit through. It doesn't simply make a show of being uncompromising – it is uncompromisingly extreme. It takes as its subject the extremes of social, cultural experience – gluttony, lust, barbarism and bad table manners. And these are the essential sensuous experiences of eating and drinking. There is a need for complementary interiors, for settings which allow these scenarios to be acted out to their most extreme.

Every day in restaurants individual dramas and traumas are acted out, if in much less horrific and exaggerated circumstances.

Eating and drinking sometimes require slow, intimate sensuous spaces, sometimes bright fast spaces. The lights, the materials, the tactility of the space create the experience. The food is the final, indispensable sensual complement.

PART 2

The idea of the city as a series of spaces for different activities, and that the restaurant and bar exist as its eating and drinking rooms, is one that Charles Baudelaire introduced in his poetry of 19th-century Paris. His text 'The Paris Spleen' refers to *flânerie*, the activity of strolling and looking around the city. The *flâneur* is the individual who carries this out: 'His passion and profession is to merge with the crowd' (Baudelaire). The activity suggests anonymity, the observer devoid of individuality. He is a man of the people, someone who exists within the urban domain. This idea has influenced the way we consider any urban space.

A walk through the city becomes a promenade. The mundane act is elevated and the space within which it occurs assumes the mantle of a theatre, the urban rooms within which activities take place taking on a more theatrical significance. To be seen in a particular place and modifying behaviour accordingly.

In this context all spaces within the city begin to take on a different significance. The library becomes the reading room, the urban park a garden, the restaurant a dining room, and the cafe a sitting room. The bar becomes a place to sit and gossip, to exchange ideas and views.

Thus defined as a platform for events, the restaurant and bar became particular scenes for the staging of performance. Being seen and becoming part of the idea of the place take on a new significance.

This conception of place, which originates in Paris, applies to the 20th-century interpretation of city. Public life has a particular significance, where you are defined by who you are. The restaurant is part of that identity. It is much more than a place to eat.

The text of James Joyce's Ulysses takes the city of Dublin as the stage for a series of narratives and events involving the life of Leopold Bloom and uses various places within the city as scenes for conversations and happenings. There is a memorable description of Bloom wandering down Grafton Street, Dublin. He is hungry and the pressure of hunger drives him into the Burton Restaurant where he is disgusted by the animal nature of eating:

THE 20TH CENTURY

Smells of men, his gorge rose Spat on sawdust, warmish cigarette smoke reek of plug spilt beer... Couldn't eat a morsel here

He backs away and decides to have a light snack at Davy Byrne's bar instead.

A cheese sandwich some olives a glass of burgundy and a light salad.

Leopold Bloom uses the city much as a *flâneur*. The interesting idea is the personal, individual experience that is portrayed in the text. The restaurant he enters and the experience he has within it are vividly and personally expressed in terms of smell, taste and the overall effect of the place. The text captures the immediacy of the scene; you could be there standing next to him. When he enters Davy Byrne's bar, the moral philosophers' bar, he is relaxed; here a more congenial atmosphere pervades. What he eats is part of the separation of the experience he has from the street. In Dublin at the beginning of the 20th century he eats olives, perhaps Spanish, drinks Burgundy – of course from France – and consumes a cheese sandwich using Gorgonzola from Italy; even Leopold Bloom had the existentialist experience, a global menu which could not have been further away from the experience of the Dublin around him.

The bar and restaurant are important rooms within the contemporary setting for the events of city life; they are part of the narrative of the place. This responds to Bernard Tschumi's idea of Event City: the city is a place for 'Events', for happenings to take place. Architecture creates the platform for these possibilities.

Dining out in a modern restaurant is an activity which conforms to fashion and at the start of the 21st century fashion is a diverse dynamic. As soon as it is defined it has moved on. It has become a never-ending re-invention of the past. The fashion of the future is an idea of the new; however, the unpredictable holds equal attraction.

Finkelstein, a sociologist, in his reflection on modern life, 'Dining Out, A Sociology of Modern Manners', describes a restaurant as a place where, *'Individuals are acting out privately held desires and needs such as the desire for entertainment, relief from boredom and the need to feel distinguished in some way.'* It is also an escape from the boredom of buying, preparing and serving food and offers a much more sociable way of eating.

In reality the commercial success of any restaurant depends on its location, street credibility and the notoriety of its chef. Many restaurants are specific to particular chefs, Rhodes in London for example. Or attached to a series of film personalities, such as Planet Hollywood, which has become a commercial enterprise. Many restaurants and bars that were once singular ventures are now part of a chain (you can never have too much of a good thing). There is more than an implication that the context of the restaurant is unimportant: it is the interior experience that provides the memory of the place. A hamburger in Times Square, New York really is the same hamburger as a hamburger in Red Square, Moscow – a sense in which taste has nothing to do with other sensory experiences. The familiarity of the food is meant to be comforting and safe in a foreign environment. Does this familiarity breed a sense of security or contempt? It does create an unnecessary homogeneity.

Less than 30 years ago taste, ingredients and food were intrinsically associated with the experience of place, as individual as the language and with all the subtleties of a dialect or local accent. Restaurants and bars are also essentially linked to the idea of place and cultural context. They define groups of people in terms of the interior spaces and use of materials and lighting and also the menu, ingredients and price.

Dining out was traditionally a very formal occasion, and certain restaurants today would have an expectation of formal rather than casual wear, but this is now the exception rather than the rule. There is a wide variety of places in any town or city which cater for all comers from casual tourists to more formal diners. The hierarchy still exists of the eater and the waiter: who is in control?

PART 3

Perhaps the most significant image of eating and drinking is that conveyed by Leonardo da Vinci's *Last Supper* (1495-8) with its immense symbolic and cultural weight, placing the individuals so as to illustrate their specific relationship to the main figure of the Christ at the centre of the table. The work creates a hierarchy of characters within the image in terms of their exact placing within the painting. It is this idea of eating and hierarchy which exists in many cultures, of the high table where elders/the elect preside over those seated at a lower level. The symbolism of the *Last Supper*, that it was a final meal, a celebration, has become elevated into ceremony. Its importance is this celebration and its particular composition of individuals.

There is a contemporary analogy to the *Last Supper*, published in *The Times* (1999), which depicts heads of large corporations including Coca-Cola and Microsoft sitting around the table in place of the disciples. Commercialism is a strong force in contemporary culture and has replaced religion in importance for most of the western world. That these media and commercial symbols have become deified to the extent that, metaphorically, they sit at the table with Christ for his Last Supper symbolises the shift of ideology at the beginning of the 21st century. Have they sold out, as Judas Iscariot did, for 30 pieces of silver for their belief in the reality around them?

The table as symbol of sharing and equality is an interesting analogy, but these new corporate deities control our every experience; they sap the individuality out of life and replace it with homogeneity - McDonald's, Coca-Cola, Microsoft. The 21st-century icons control ever more. The sense of local culture is being eroded by these global concepts; indeed, they contribute to the suppression of local culture and expression.

The interior space of a restaurant has a quality of fantasy. It is definitely an interior space, something which has to be entered and experienced; one has to cross over the threshold from the exterior world to the interior, moving from reality to a place of fantasy. A restaurant or bar has the possibility to be anything

HYPER REAL

or to use any reference, it is part of our world of entertainment and leisure. Here we come to be amused and excited, even shocked; we want to be transported from the banality of everyday urban existence.

The architecture of the bar and restaurant is not a sincere one of form and function but of form and fun. If the referent is the Renaissance then the experience of the space can be flamboyant and colourful; if it is a modern interior then the mood can be cool and hard. There are no programmatic restrictions; to be successful the space has to excite or challenge.

It is an architecture of surface at its most ultimate where mirrored glass can appear to extend volumes of space; here illusion is important, even critical. In experiencing these spaces we can question what is real. French sociologist Jean Baudrillard argues that the definition of the real is that which it is possible to give an equivalent reproduction. In the new world of hyper-reality, spectacle has replaced the real.

On the nature of hyper-reality

For bar and restaurant design the idea of imitation/simulation of other existing environments is synonymous with the concept of theatre. Accepted everyday life phenomena are conscripted to a new meta-reality of escapist reality. Umberto Eco and Jean Baudrillard enunciated such theories in their writings, respectively, on travels in hyper-reality and simulacra and simulation. In these theories the referent of a design becomes, as it were, disconnected from the ultimate proposal, taking on a life of its own, departing from that to which it initially referred. In such cases the artificial reality takes on its own independent existence and, so to speak, is able to jettison the reality to which it initially related. In Baudrillard's terminology the architecture of bars and restaurants adopts its own hyper-real presence.

As people who experience such environments we in effect consume an artifice for our own hedonistic purposes and enter into a fantasy, accepting a sanitised replica world of reality. As such, we knowingly abandon our educated judgement for that of a fantasy: in the pursuit of entertainment, we buy into a

Disneyland world and we leave behind our everyday circumspection in favour of an all-powerful meta-reality. This is an experience of theatre, of suspended disbelief where, upon an artificial stage, we become performers of our own innermost desires in a venue of our own choosing.

The choice of such a fantasy world need not accord to some prescribed hegemony, but as we move from bar to bar, can accommodate itself to a variety of tastes, aspirations and notions of pleasure. As consumers we become hedonistic chameleons in an artificial world of social proclivity. Bars and restaurants are the theatres for such engagement.

At Trinity University Dublin there is a Georgian building, one of many there designed by Cassells. Here within a small room off the fellows room one has a quite unexpected experience. From the 18th-century interior one steps into a room which is part of the 20th century. A step from the relative past to the relative future. But this is a very specific room; it is a replica of the Adolf Loos bar, the original of which exists in Vienna.

The original bar sits off a side street in Vienna. It is relatively low with a bar on the left side as you enter. It is in effect a small intimate room with several seats at the bar and a series of small circular tables with seating around the walls. The tables have light fittings set beneath a glass surface to create an ethereal glow around those sitting and drinking.

The bar in Dublin (by Architects De Blacam and Meagher) is exact except for one twist, it is a reverse or mirrored copy. This seems a subtle twist as the bar is covered from eye level to ceiling level with mirrors that gives an impression of infinite repeated space; the mirrored impression of the room seems a further exaggeration of this idea.

So how can an experience created by Adolf Loos in Vienna at the beginning of the 20th century exist in Dublin in a late 17th-century building? It is a seeming contradiction that further substantiates the idea of the hyper real. Once you step over the threshold of the room you have already engaged in the game. You have moved from reality to fantasy.

PART 4

THE FLEXIBLE INTERIOR

The temporary nature of the interior of a contemporary bar or restaurant is indicative of the changing, almost fickle attitude of individuals to styles and themes. Restaurants have to be fashionable places with food and interiors to match and, like fashion, last year's chic is definitely not in vogue this year. The interior space is like a suit of clothes or a skirt; it is superficial and can be peeled off and re-invented at will.

Restaurant style and interior space are highly commercial and have to be flexible. Many restaurant spaces are renovations, existing in buildings which were once something else, and use the references around them to stimulate a design. Banks, even industrial buildings that have become obsolete have been regenerated to capture new meaning in the 20th-century townscape.

An example of this is the Dublin Morrison hotel which opened in 1999 and incorporates bars and restaurants on its site along the quayside on the north bank of the River Liffey. The idea of the interior skin of the building being analogous to a set of clothes is apposite here: the restaurant has been designed by architects Donahue Wallace together with John Rocha, fashion designer. The building itself is a contradiction: an 18th-century facade fronts a new building built behind. It is eclectic in its references both in terms of style and materials. The base of the building is grey Portuguese limestone with grey granite. 'The interior references are derived from a notion of East meets West while borrowing language from the East, very much contemporary Ireland.' This is taken from the promotional material provided by the hotel and indicates an unexpected melange of references.

Thinking of the rooms as interior skins, like suits of clothes that can be easily detached and re-invented at will, is similar to the dictates of high fashion in Paris, Milan, New York. Each season brings new references, interpretations, suggestions. Nothing is fixed. To consider a restaurant in this way allows changes in culinary taste to be easily reflected. In the Morrison bar one experiences chic minimalism. There is a connection to the outside – the bar is elevated from the street affording a wonderful view of the River Liffey and Dublin's new footbridge. It is a crossroads in the city where north meets south. A place to see and be seen.

Moving into the building there is a precision in the materiality and detailing. In contrast the experience of the restaurant provides more intimate, less intimidating spaces. The coolness of the bar is replaced by subtle lighting and beautiful art objects which create a very particular experience. The materials are very soft and textured – an unexpected and successful contrast. The juxtaposition of bar and restaurant in this context demonstrates the differences between their functions, the difference between the collective social activity of drinking and the more formal, sometimes intimate and sensuous experience of eating.

Large restaurant spaces have generated a very different character of restaurant and eating experience from the traditional intimate candle lit dinner. Examples of this might be Mezzo in London or Paris. In this commercial world of eating, in an evening these large eating halls may have two sittings for dinner to capitalise on their popularity. In this circumstance, there is more pressure attached to the process of eating; it becomes less of an event.

The transformation of interior space is put to dramatic effect by Peter Meacock at the Severnshed, Bristol with the use of the bar as moving element. This goes beyond the abstract idea of inserting a bar as 'a piece of furniture' within the space. Here the bar is something physically different from the surrounding space, a service element as a moving object or vehicle, allowing bar and restaurant to function as the ultimately flexible interior. Here an innovative approach to design is facilitated by the use of mechanical systems normally found in industry. The stainless steel bar hovers using air film technology which means that the floor surface underneath is undamaged. In terms of restaurant use, the space can be divided in many ways or left clear to accommodate large functions. This results in a space which constantly re-invents itself.

PART 5

A process of globalisation is occurring in our eating and drinking habits and there is also a great deal written about healthy eating that promotes organic and natural foods. Cuisine has also moved into the realm of art with the chef perceived as the artist creating his piece for consumption.

The idea that our diet now includes local produce and restaurants should offer a typical British menu has been overtaken by the wide availability of different foods and ingredients all year round. Moreover, the population is widely travelled and their palate has broadened to enjoy and expect flavours and food from around the world. This has created a pluralism in eating and restaurants: specialised restaurants exist in any city high street to provide food from anywhere in the world. The tapas bar, the curry house, the pizza parlour, provide a particular experience of food and surroundings designed to create the illusion of being somewhere else ... In reality the foods we eat - chilli con carne from Texas, vichyssoise from France - are reinterpretations of an original. Authenticity has become difficult to define, but it may now be irrelevant. The interior styles which these restaurants present are intrinsically attached to the food and sometimes have the same problem. The result is a hybrid of styles and references to match the ingredients on the menu.

A sort of critical regionalism associated with cooking has developed over the past decade, the notion that place has a particularity of experience and culture attached to it. This in itself creates an expectation of experience. These preconceptions of experience have affected the nature of the architecture with which the interior space and food type are associated. There is an expectation that a French restaurant will evoke an idea or understanding of place. To eat French food you must be removed from the reality of Britain to an interpretation of a French restaurant with music, lighting and French waiters to complete the illusion. This is an approach which Conran, with his distinctive attitude towards Mediterranean life

and cooking, has encouraged. Fifteen years ago the idea of foreign cuisine would have been limited on the British high street to French or Italian as this was the physical limit of most people's experience - and equally the limit of their imagination.

This fantastical voyage into an imagined culinary zone is one experience of a restaurant interior; another is to take an existing building or location and use its originality of place, context or form to create a specific architecture. Bibendum does this using the Michelin Building as a reference around which the whole restaurant is designed: the building gives the restaurant its identity. Equally the Oxo Tower is an important symbol and reference on the London skyline and has transformed itself into a chic location, the place to be seen or to look out from.

The idea that food should also be fast and constantly available anytime, anywhere has moved us away from indigenous eating styles and habits. Takeaway foods such as the hamburger and pizza have changed our eating habits in a global way as well as having corporate images attached to them. Fast food is a phenomenon that has created a different sort of eating place, a hybrid, halfway between a restaurant and a sandwich bar which accommodates the speed of modern life. We have fast food, brasserie style bars, traditional pub food all alongside representatives of every area of the former British empire, as well as venues with European menus. Chinese, Italian, Greek, Turkish, Vietnamese, Thai, Japanese: this variety can be found in any major European or international city. It is not surprising that this melange of food and cultures has spawned a diverse and exciting collection of architectural and interior styles. The possibility of mixing cross-culturally is a phenomenon with which Philippe Starck has experimented. The Asia de Cuba bar at St Martins Hotel, London crosses Asian and South American cuisine, and allows the interior a life of its own. Here an unexpected fusion of ingredients has directly affected the invention of the interior. The restaurant's signature dish is 'Szechuan

GLOBALISATION

Peppercorn Crusted Tuna with Boniato Mash and Citrus Ponzu'. What an evocative brief for an interior!

We are witnessing a new flavour in interior architecture, one born of the mixture of culinary references. There is no limit to the possibilities. The future of the bar and restaurant in the life of the city is secure and central regardless of the burgeoning of information technology. Particularly in our stressful contemporary society we are increasingly drawn to engage in escapism in a fantastical place created in the mind of architect or designer. A different kind of virtual reality.

We have an intrinsic need to meet new people, experience new tastes and to drink and eat together. These are essential sensuous experiences we cannot deny ourselves and together they form and define the culture of a place. If we stop participating, culture stops too.

The restaurant and bar provide the opportunity for that unscripted encounter, an unknown possibility, to satiate desires, to meet new people, savour new tastes. Making an entrance through the doors of a bar is like coming on a stage to participate in a new scene with unknown characters, the more bizarre and eccentric the stage set, the better. In a bar you can re-invent yourself and become part of the scene. By comparison a restaurant experience is more anticipated, more considered, the characters more familiar, the environment and mood more formal. The idea of place is totally disconnected from life outside the restaurant door; once you step over the threshold the fantasy begins – the menu, furniture, lighting, the spaces create the ensemble.

Perhaps a template for bar design could be that provided for Astika and Pleven by Graham Noble Associates. They have designed a portable bar such that it can be lifted up and transported to any location. It renders the idea of context completely irrelevant. Site doesn't matter as long as you have a bar where you can have a party in the middle of any urban square or street, instant social mixing. It is the idea of the hamburger van translated into drinking, an object that creates an immediate 'event' or happening in the centre of any city, the most temporary non-contextual experience possible.

The future of bar and restaurant design involves a continual response to fashion, which has no feeling of place. To react to cultural and social conditions, to be fast where speed is necessary and slow where time is less important. The way we eat and drink is directly and immediately affected by our life experiences, and the places in which we meet to eat and drink are becoming more and more important social centres. They may yet become the main arena for people to engage with one another as the technological revolution of digital communication and computers makes us ever more isolated. They will continue to be the backdrop to our leisure world, a world of fantasy and escapism. Where the experience, the theatre is everything. Step over the threshold and engage in the non-reality.

References
'The Cook, the thief, his wife and her lover'.
Peter Greenaway (1984)
Bernard Tschumi, 'Event City', (1984) MIT
James Joyce, 'Ulysses', (1934) Random House

Bibliography
Finkelstein J: *Dining Out: a Sociology of Modern Manners*, (1989) Cambridge
Umberto Eco: *Travels in Hyperreality*, (1987) Picador
Walter Benjamin: *Charles Baudelaire*, (1977) Verso Books
J Baudrillard: *Simulation*, New York, (1983) Semiotext

astro bar

LOCATION: REYKJAVIK, ICELAND
ARCHITECT/DESIGNER: MICHAEL YOUNG, MY STUDIO LTD, REYKJAVIK, ICELAND

The project entailed the refurbishment of one of Reykjavik's oldest buildings (also its oldest club and name). Unfortunately, much of the building was protected by law, even though it is only 90 years old. In fact, it's a bit of a standing joke because it's not that special. There was not a straight line anywhere so that the Studio's first task was to sort out the geometry to create a workable environment. The design did not envisage remote control ceilings and lighting systems like some clubs ... it's very much more street than that. The building is treated more as a reflection of the designer's general approach than as a single piece of architecture.

The client is young and enthusiastic with an understanding of their own generation. Theirs is basically a DJ club with four bars and two dance floors, a fun house and it is the fun element that the designer has tried to reflect when creating the appropriate atmosphere in different areas.

The starting point was observing Icelandic craftsmanship. Their craftsmen are extremely enthusiastic and skilled, especially at concrete and steel work that is used a lot in swimming pools and geothermal areas in Iceland. The design is an amalgam of a sort of swimming pool and picnic area concept and was carried out with the assistance of a local company responsible for building work in the Blue Lagoon, a local geothermal pool. It is a daring attempt to bring a little bit of the outdoors indoors since Iceland can be so cold and windy. A unique creation.

Cappellini made the furniture and Sawaya & Moroni made special pieces for the project. These surround the central Smarty pool for the sitter to gaze on before entry. Lighting was manufactured by Eurolounge and included the manufacture of some old-fashioned woven steel lights to help evoke an artificial aspect. Corona provided all the bar surfaces and shelves. The atmosphere is cutting edge, surreal. Almost like stepping into the virtual.

Upstairs a rather different atmosphere is evident, much more relaxed and peaceful. It has an ambient floor created by Jeremy Lord; it also contains the Red Room, a private members' area. Thermo formed walls contain a lighting system that reacts to movement, starting at pale pink and becoming deeper red in response to physical activity. A reactive environment.

MICHAEL YOUNG, MY STUDIO LTD

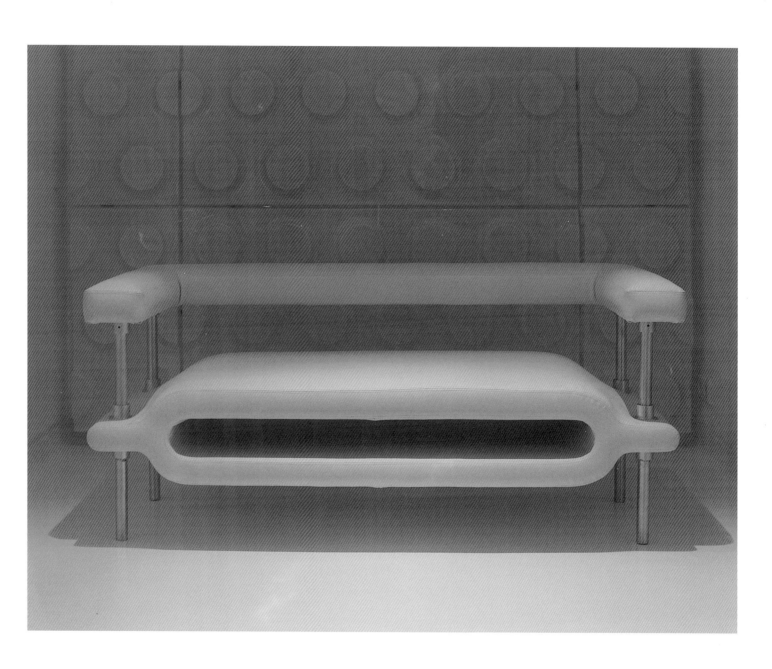

MICHAEL YOUNG, MY STUDIO LTD

aureole

LOCATION: **LAS VEGAS, USA**
ARCHITECT/DESIGNER: **TIHANY DESIGN, NEW YORK, USA**

Aureole Las Vegas is Adam D. Tihany's salute to chef Charlie Palmer's multifaceted talents. Tihany has often said that the only way to truly know a chef is to taste his cooking and he is renowned for creating an interior that perfectly reflects an owner's sensibilities. Charlie Palmer's cuisine ranges from the casual yet sophisticated to the formal yet warm and comfortable – which Tihany has expertly presented through design.

Stepping through the main entrance on to a glass walkway at the second storey of a four-storey tower, one is thrust into this exciting and stimulating space. An awesome glass and steel wine tower soars to the sky lit ceiling. An interactive sculpture, this great centrepiece is both architecture and theatre. Like a scene from *Mission Impossible*, this wine tower is actually a restaurant's wine cellar and the stewards must strap themselves into steel cabled harnesses, which will take them up and down the tower to select their bottles. Surrounding the base of this tower is the bar/lounge area, a perfect vantage point to watch the action from a comfortable clubby atmosphere.

Passing from the lounge into the main dining room Tihany allows the dining experience to become the show. A contemporary room, its sleek style befits chef Palmer's exceptional cuisine. The ambience is sophisticated but with a definitive air of comfort. The materials are fanciful and put to innovative uses. Of exceptional interest are the intricate ceiling and custom designed lighting by Tihany. The fascinating and magnificent free-form works of one of the world's premier glass artists, Luiano Vistosi, are placed throughout the room as soft, ethereal visions. The ambience of this main dining room is ingeniously carried into the large private dining room which can also be divided into three separate private dining areas.

Towards the back of the main dining room another most intriguing structure acts as the entrance to the Auriole Swan Court, the most formal of Aureole Las Vegas' dining experiences. Water cascades over a glass doorway to give the impression of stepping through a waterfall to enter a beautiful room of luxury and elegance. From the custom designed graphic carpet to the silver leaf concave arched ceiling, this fine dining area exudes warmth and elegance conveyed through the use of the richest of materials and detailing. The space allows for an intimate dining experience in either high backed banquettes or tables bordering the terrace and surrounding lake.

Tihany's design of Aureole Las Vegas is a spectacular expression of restaurant as theatre and Charlie Palmer's cuisine as the star.

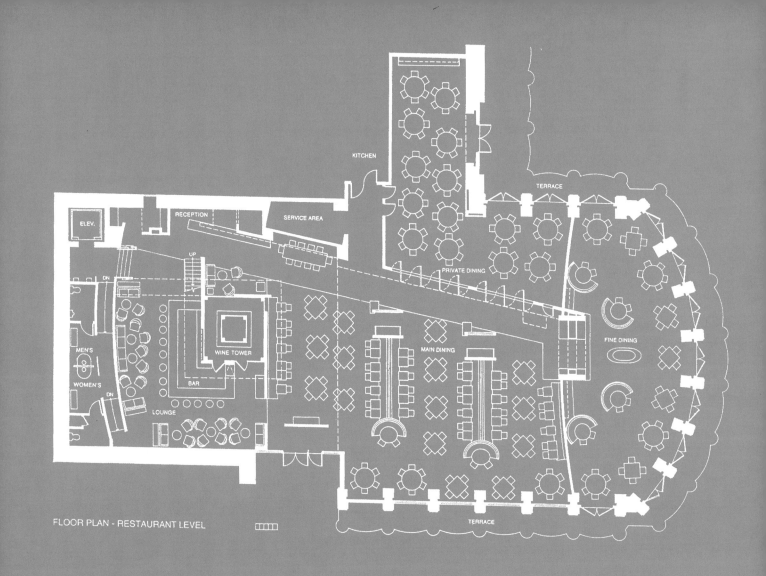

ELEV.

RECEPTION

SERVICE AREA

KITCHEN

TERRACE

DN

UP

MEN'S

WOMEN'S

DN

WINE TOWER

BAR

PRIVATE DINING

LOUNGE

MAIN DINING

FINE DINING

FLOOR PLAN - RESTAURANT LEVEL

TERRACE

TIHANY DESIGN

babe ruth's

LOCATION: LONDON, UK
ARCHITECT/DESIGNER: BARR GAZETAS, LONDON, UK

This bar cum restaurant is situated at first-floor level overlooking the Finchley Road.

The kitchen area is thrust forward to centre stage. The design concept is of 'cooking as theatre' with all of the kitchen staff visible from the atrium. Adding a strongly youthful and energetic feel, a 'one on one' basketball court has been provided to give customers the opportunity to play basketball after eating.

A ramped public route made from English oak boards and Portuguese limestone has been created allowing access to the different zones: the bar, games area and functions room. Raised banquettes and stainless steel sofas add to the variety of seating options with most seats having views to the kitchen.

TV monitors are distributed around the interior with a large projection screen in the main body of the restaurant. Scenes have been set for mood music and lighting at different times of the day. Fibre optic lighting has been used behind the bar to create a constantly changing colour wall and illumination for the names of sport stars that are carved out of the rendered bar-front.

People approaching along the Finchley Road have a view straight into the heart of the restaurant. This opportunity has been exploited by the provision of phosphorescent rear illuminated signage to the street, illuminated ceiling 'clouds' made of rubber, a mural, and the positioning of the stainless steel sofas to give high external visibility.

backflip

LOCATION: SAN FRANCISCO, USA
ARCHITECT/DESIGNER: FUN DISPLAY, SAN FRANCISCO, USA

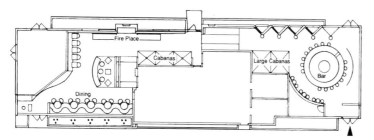

Backflip, adjacent to the chic Phoenix Hotel at 601 Eddy Street in San Francisco, opened in May 1997. Fun Display designed the restaurant and lounge as an aquatic themed utopia that is both visually stimulating and hypnotic. The 4000 square foot space is divided into two rooms. The dining room is in a poolside palette of aqua, cobalt blue and chartreuse. Inspired by the Phoenix's courtyard pool, the room evokes a retro '60s beach club culture. Fabulous fabrics such as lamé, and chenille, weird vinyls, metallic leather, mesh netting and blue faux fur are combined with curved frosted custom glass screens, mirrors, steel, custom designed fibreglass chairs and five spouting fountains to help create a Miami-esque über-lounge.

The bar area is an oasis of cobalt blue, its curved glass walls embracing a circular mirrored bar. The back bar is a circular stack of liquor bottles topped with a fountain. Bar stools are metallic blue leather and all other furniture and treatments are cobalt blue. The whole room is then bathed in blue light creating an effect like taking a high dive into a deep pool.

The owners of Backflip wanted to reinvent the 1960s cocktail party, transforming it into a new type of '90s dining experience now known as 'New Cocktail Cuisine'. Diners can pick at food from dim-sum type carts and enjoy their meal in casual living room settings or outdoors at the poolside. More traditional seating is available in private câbanas or at fountainside tables.

BACKFLIP

FUN DISPLAY

bargo

LOCATION: GLASGOW, UK
ARCHITECT/DESIGNER: BRANSON COATES ARCHITECTURE LTD, LONDON, UK

Bargo is Branson Coates' massive new bar on Albion Street
for Bass Taverns/Tennents in Glasgow.

The design exploits to the full the surprise of the triple
height space of the former cheese market building, with seating
on two levels served and serviced from behind a curved open
screen of over scaled timbers that extends from floor to roof.
This outward facing arc of dockside detail – greenish light
penetrating through portholes, ships' glimmering copper
and steel plates – is reflected back in angled fragments from
the huge suspended mirror up and back of it, and topped by
an opalescent resin light wall that creates an over-scaled
focus for the whole space. In daytime the lighting is strong,
natural light entering from top and side; at night this changes
to the underwater glimmer of reflected dockside factory lights.
This dual identity is exaggerated by hoisting the suspended
canopy at night, lowering it by day.

Materials are chosen to give a friendly industrial atmosphere
with red oxide steel and timber structures; metal strapped
timber banquette dividers call to mind shipping crates. Behind
the hand made, zinc topped, copper fronted bar, and enhancing
the nautical theme, are brushed stainless steel panels set with
finely polished old aluminium portholes. The bar itself addresses
both inside and outside by means of its sliding glass frontage.

Nigel Coates' Bargo beech wood chairs and tables take
a coltish stance – the chairs' metallic upholstery and gun-metal
blue steel, the three tables' zinc tops are suited equally to
daytime sunshine or night-time's greenish glow.

44　　　　　　　　　　　　BRANSON COATES ARCHITECTURE LTD

bierodrome

LOCATION: **LONDON, UK**
ARCHITECT/DESIGNER: **BUSHE ASSOCIATES LIMITED, LONDON, UK**

Tim Bushe Associates was approached in November 1998, with a view to realising a new concept for a Bierodrome bar/restaurant on Upper Street, Islington.

Considered as three distinct areas, bar/restaurant/beer hall, each zone has its own identity but all are linked by continuous elements that include polished concrete flooring and unique light fittings. The interior comprises two eccentric arched vaults spanning the length of the building on the ground floor, forming the letter 'B' on its side profiles. Behind the facade at ground level is a bar, obscured from the exterior of the building by a full height, internally illuminated translucent Reglit glass wall. To the left of this bar, a beer hall extends to bathroom facilities at the rear of the building. The rear of the beer hall can be closed off for private parties by pulling across a cowhide curtain. On the right hand side, the bar and lounge area are separated from the restaurant zone at the rear by kitchen facilities and a serving counter. The rear wall, visible to the public, is also a Reglit glass screen, which provides a glowing sea-green background for the whole interior.

Baronial style light fittings and a roaring 'love' fire complement the subterranean atmosphere created by the use of dark wood panelling and Jacobean oak for tables and stools. A double height lounge space between the front bar area and the beer hall has a consciously après-ski feel with a rolled leather sofa facing on to the artificial log gas fireplace. Daylight is introduced into the vaulted halls and to the double height lounge through slits, which at night are illuminated by hidden strip lights. Tim Bushe Associates designed the contemporary 'wagon wheel chandelier' using rolled steel sections hung on stainless steel wires with projecting halogen bulbs. These can be dimmed to provide variable light, from brilliant white to glowing amber.

The shop front is fully glazed in three equal bays. The first offers a view into the timbered beer hall while the end bay creates the entrance with views into the dining hall beyond. The central bay is filled with a 2.8 metre high 2.2 metre wide display, formed by 200 bottles suspended in beer coloured resin blocks. The Reglit screen behind contains an opening in which sits a solitary bottle suspended in resin symbolising the 201 different Belgian beers on offer at the bar. Reinforcing Belgo's particular brand of humour, there is a strong graphic/wordplay element in the beer hall where Belgian slang words are printed into the timber light slots; in the toilets 2.5 metre high cubicle doors contain oversized cow photographs. A further large cow image above the urinals includes the caption 'Belgium has the world's only fully illuminated motorway system, which can be seen from space' - food for thought.

circus

LOCATION: **LONDON, UK**
ARCHITECT/DESIGNER: **DAVID CHIPPERFIELD ARCHITECTS, LONDON, UK**

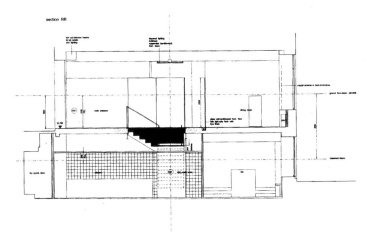

This restaurant and bar is located in a former television studio near Golden Square in Soho, London.

The restaurant occupies the ground floor and is naturally lit through large steel windows on three sides. This space is designed in the spirit of a classic dining room. There are as few service facilities as possible; those necessaries are contained in a group of illuminated glass boxes constructed of glass sandwich panels silk-screened with different translucent colours before being laminated. The windows are screened with a 'box of light', two screens of translucent voile. The floor is made of wenge timber. Tables are clothed, and chairs designed by David Chipperfield are upholstered in a mushroom tone.

The cocktail bar in the basement is split over two levels. One arrives at the upper level, which is given over to a large U-shaped bar, reflecting the arrangement of deep beams in the ceiling. The lower level of the bar, where people are able to sit in groups, looks over a small landscaped courtyard filled with bamboo and pebbles. This long room is furnished with a series of large square ottomans and tables. The long wall opposite the courtyard is clad with black Vitrolite glass and mirrors.

All kitchen and storage facilities are housed in the basement. The public toilets have black granite floors, black Vitrolite glass walls and wenge-panelled cubicles.

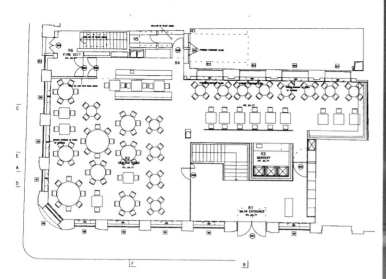

DAVID CHIPPERFIELD ARCHITECTS

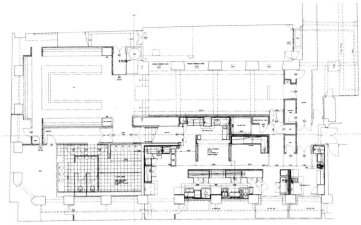

le cirque 2000

LOCATION: **NEW YORK, USA**
ARCHITECT/DESIGNER: **TIHANY DESIGN, NEW YORK, USA**

Design for Le Cirque 2000 demanded Tihany's own high wire act while installing Sirio Maccioni's 'circus' in the landmark Villard House at the New York Palace Hotel.

The programme could have gone along with the existing interiors to create a period piece, a beautiful, elegant and totally intimidating experience. Instead it was decided to meticulously restore the existing architectural features to act as a backdrop to updated, fanciful furnishings. The contemporary elements would provide an innovative vantage point from which to view the original architecture. For the designers, the prospect of creating tension between the two worlds was exciting. They worked on the premise that the juxtaposition of these two worlds would prove mutually enhancing. Among the public there are those who agree, and those who disagree - either way, the space evokes strong reactions; the perfect circus for Sirio.

The restrictions inherent in the building's landmark status forbade the piercing of walls, floors or ceilings. Turning this restriction into an asset, the solution was to treat this august space as if a circus had been unpacked inside it. A back lit, freestanding bar structure was installed that includes three elliptical tochere towers. A clock on a wire travels between the towers and two neon ellipses. All of the furnishings within the restaurant - cocktail tables, club chairs, wing chairs, dining chairs, banquettes, even carpets and china - were designed specifically for no specific space. No shape, no colour was too bold. In the front dining room etched-glass screens with inset stained glass circus balls were brought in to offset the period murals. High backed, purple and teal one armed chairs with clown button details down their backs dance about the room. In the Hunt Room, originally too dark to comfortably serve dinner, new light sources were created. Striped light towers emanating from the red and yellow leather banquettes provide the solution. The brightness of the upholstery and new lighting treatments turn an old dark panelled room into a bright fun space.

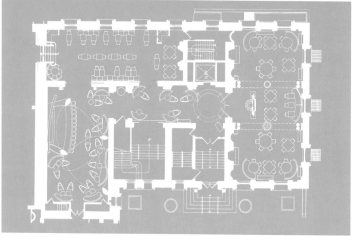

NON · EST · IMPERANDVM · CITO · ENIM · EXHAVRIET · ILLOS · NVNOVAM ·

the elbow room

LOCATION: LEEDS, UK
ARCHITECT/DESIGNER: PAUL DALY DESIGN STUDIO, LONDON, UK

Housed in the old Music Factory (home to the Back to Basics club), this site proved an ambitious project. The venue is spread over two floors and accommodates 18 pool tables. The Elbow Room is following what seems to be a burgeoning trend – the club-like place that isn't a club. Targeting an older clientele it aims to provide a civilised alternative to the frenzy of traditional nightclubs.

Located on the second and third floors of the old Music Factory building in Call Lane, Leeds, home of the original Back to Basics headquarters, Elbow Room is a 10,000 square foot venue. The original factory ceiling heights were quite low with each floor sharply cut off from the next, so a single space was created by cutting out and making a mezzanine of the third floor. This opening is pierced by the now famous screen-tower/back bar, which stands about 20 feet high.

Upon entering the venue on the second floor patrons immediately get the feel of the whole space because of the cut out. The dance floor is right beside the bar and directly below the mezzanine above, creating a demography of performer and audience. The furniture, both fixed and free standing, is all site specific.

The pool canopies are of particular interest due to their sculptural integrity and functionality. The fixtures and fittings have developed to respond to the spaces. The ceiling has a loft appearance; old reinforcement joists are clad in rated plasterboard and painted chocolate brown and sandstone. The intention is to create a subdued effect punctuated by detail.

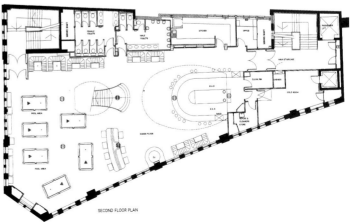

SECOND FLOOR PLAN

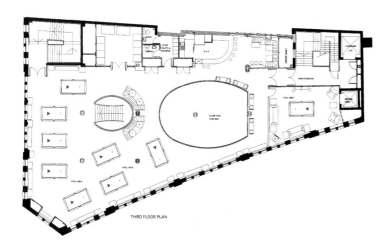

THIRD FLOOR PLAN

PAUL DALY DESIGN STUDIO

the eyre brothers

LOCATION: LONDON UK
ARCHITECT/DESIGNER: WAUGH THISTLETON, LONDON, UK

The new Eyre Brothers restaurant takes the existing concrete frame building as a backdrop for the activity within. The original manufacturing function of the building is echoed in the production of the kitchen and the bar while the new activity is introduced by the insertion of a strong architectural element.

The service areas are characterised by glaringly hygienic surfaces – stainless steel, white body glass; lighting is functional and bright. In contrast, the dining area is composed of warm, sustainable hardwoods, with furniture and fittings in leather, bronze and coloured glass. Minimal diffuse lighting complements the light that spills out from the bar.

The dining space is encircled and defined by the jojoba hardwood boards that wrap around the end walls and ceiling. This timber envelope does not enclose the space but creates a stage set, presenting a theatre to the street and to the waiters behind. Similarly, the 20 metre long bar leading into the open kitchen provides a constant performance for the diners.

The restaurant is about two environments, making and consuming, the distinct experiences of preparing food and eating. Each is provided with its own customised architecture and each is a profound expression of its function. The dynamic from the space results from this polarity.

In designing a chair for the Eyre Brothers restaurant, the aim was to produce a contemporary piece of furniture with a classic and timeless simplicity. The inspiration for the form can be found in the classic 19th-century American library chair and in the 1950s Cipriani chair, from Harry's Bar in Venice.

The simple function of the dining chair is to be able to support both a dining and reclining position in comfort. The contemporary nature of the chair is found in the expression of the function and in the ergonomy of the design.

The partnership worked closely with the manufacturer, Englender, using their knowledge of joinery and modern computer routing techniques to produce a highly crafted and engineered solution. The frame becomes a precise expression of both the human and structural requirements of the chair.

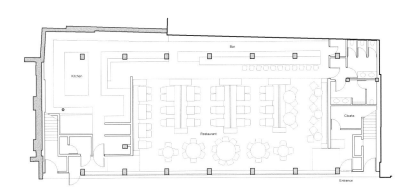

WAUGH THISTLETON

WAUGH THISTLETON

georges

LOCATION: PARIS, FRANCE
ARCHITECT/DESIGNER: JAKOB + MACFARLANE, PARIS, FRANCE

This restaurant sits inside a familiar, perhaps iconic piece of 20th-century architecture, the Centre Pompidou. The brief was to design a restaurant on the sixth floor that opened out on to an exterior terrace. The problem was how to respond to such a particular architectural context. The architects were interested in producing an architecture that was made from what existed: not in importing or creating by addition, but in proposing the lightest possible intervention. The idea was to discover or insert a kind of non-existent or background presence - at an extreme, a non-architectural or non-designed response. This led to the idea of working with the floor, proposing this surface as a new field of intervention. It was deformed in such a way that a series of volumes could be inserted underneath, creating a new landscape with interior and exterior conditions, a hidden camouflaged experience.

The floor or skin is made out of aluminium, a material which when brushed absorbs and reflects light, reinforcing the notion of background: appearance and disappearance. A minimal material presence with a strong personality, it creates a kind of mask.

A series of different functional areas slid beneath the skin: kitchen, bar, coat store, reception room. Each finds their own form through the process of design. The project was then finalised at a moment in time, caught or frozen in a state of movement. The architect's intention was to create an architecture that records the dynamic of programme and actuality.

The original building grid provided the reference and this was then deformed by volumes or pockets of space.

Another response to the building was to work with the principle that all fluids arrive via the ceiling and then descend into each pocket. With the Pompidou as host, each of the four pockets has its own systems for ventilation and the delivery of water and electricity. Water acts as a sort of life support system. This was part of the intention to return to the building's system in order to have a dialogue with it, referencing its original construction ideas of changeability, flexible systems, spontaneous systems, performance.

The furniture has been designed so that all pieces are aligned 70 centimetres off the floor in order to create a sea of furniture, allowing outside space to seamlessly join with inside space. Steel and soft polyurethane are the materials employed as they can be easily moulded and formed to create the dynamic space required.

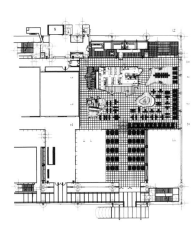

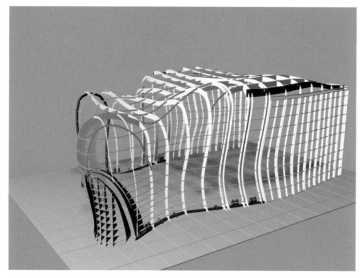
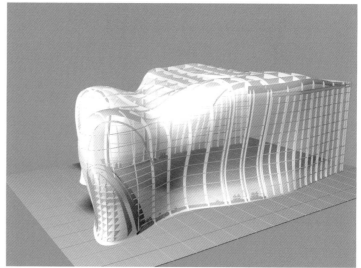
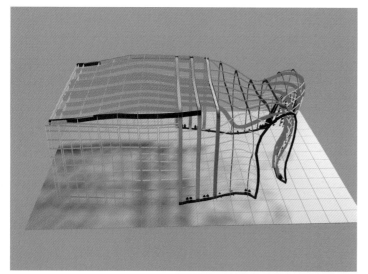
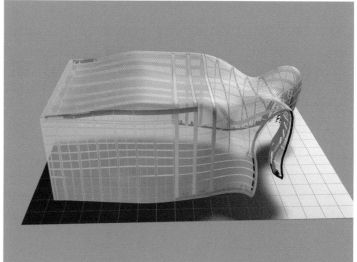
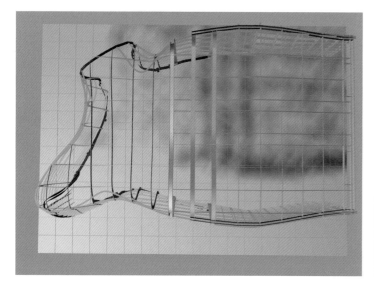
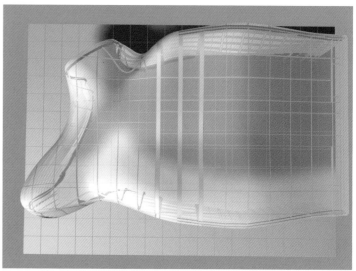

JAKOB + MACFARLANE

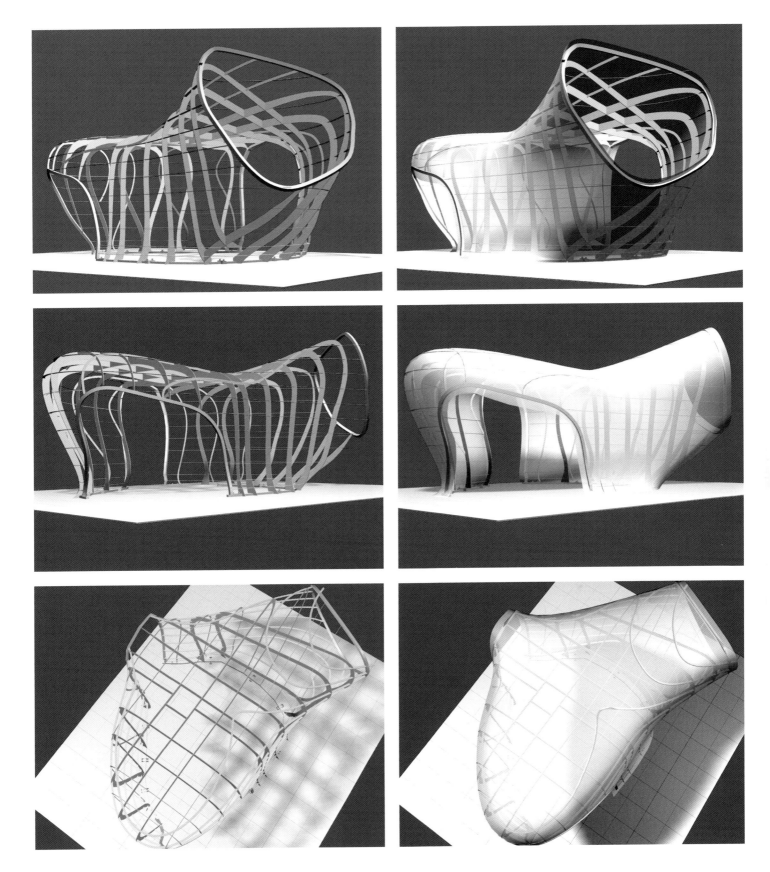

JAKOB + MACFARLANE

grand central

LOCATION: LONDON, UK
ARCHITECT/DESIGNER: GRAEME WILLIAMSON AND ZOË SMITH, BLOCK ARCHITECTURE, LONDON, UK

The principle behind the design of Grand Central was to make physical the movement and dynamism which bind the static and architectural elements of the city, to create a space which uses light, movement and electricity as physical building elements rather than simply to apply a new architectural surface to an existing one. The bar is situated on a busy road junction in Shoreditch and the aim was to draw the dynamic exterior conditions into the interior of the space.

The proposals for the bar drew directly from this context of road junctions, traffic lights and city movement, conditions which stimulated the idea of tapping into the external ebb and flow while simultaneously providing a retreat from the perpetual 'stop, wait and go' punctuation of urban life. The bar's name, taken from New York's metropolitan hub train station, was inspired primarily by the dimensions of the space. Its scale, at 5 metres high, along with the building's large windows, has the feel of a train station or other public space where there is continuous motion.

To realise these ideas in physical terms the architects have drawn on influences from long exposure/night photography of traffic movement and frozen this into interior wall surfaces within the bar. They have constructed 'lightstream' walls, suggestive of this movement and flow, which draw people in from the street and into the centre of the space. The walls are manufactured from strips of live edge, and coloured Perspex laminated together and lit from behind to create an extruded light path giving the impression of car headlights and tail lights. Accentuating this motion of the walls is a lighting rig which starts as 10 lines at the entry door and then spreads through the space to the dining area where it becomes 10 lines again. The ring was manufactured on site using galvanised steel conduiting and junction boxes and has similarities to a circuit diagram, train tracks or tram systems in plan. Each node has a downlight and red LED in a grid to develop the idea of traffic systems further.

All the furniture was also designed by the architects, including translucent resin table tops, WC sinks and urinal (lit from underneath) and the wall mounted light diffusers in the tiled interior of the 'subterranean' WC entrance space. The chairs in the central space are standard polyprops modified to be made with perforated leather padded seats and seat backs and grey powder coated legs. The chairs and stools on the upper levels were designed using the same perforated leather which is again repeated on the upholstered booth seating on the raised levels.

GRAEME WILLIAMSON AND ZOË SMITH, BLOCK ARCHITECTURE

GRAEME WILLIAMSON AND ZOË SMITH, BLOCK ARCHITECTURE

gravity

LOCATION: **DUBLIN , REPUBLIC OF IRELAND**
ARCHITECT/DESIGNER: **RKD ARCHITECTS, DUBLIN, REPUBLIC OF IRELAND**

Developed in 1904 as one of the first steel-framed buildings in Europe, the newly refurbished Guinness Storehouse encompasses gallery and exhibition areas, event venues, a visitor experience, the company archive; training and conference facilities and restaurants and bars. The 170 square foot building runs over six storeys and is built around a carved out, circular atrium.

Located on the additional seventh floor, perched on top of the Storehouse, is Dublin's newest pub – Gravity – which appears to hover atop the building and is accessed from the sixth floor by means of a panoramic glass lift. Designed by Dublin architects RKD, it is an entirely new circular structure, also steel-framed, with a floor to ceiling glazed perimeter. This offers breathtaking 360 degree views of the city of Dublin and surrounding countryside and, being the highest elevation in the capital, the spectator's view is completely unobstructed. It provides a window to city life both day and night. This bar is definitely a spectator bar to sit in and look out. It contrasts to the traditional Irish bar which is in a closed room to keep out the weather. Modern contemporary Irish and European in ambience, the bar provides an exciting experience and the sort of stunning views previously only dreamt of.

Materials and furniture are both contemporary, with mirrors on tabletops used to reflect light and curvaceous 'Swan' chairs designed by Arne Jacobsen. The furniture is predominantly deep blue and provides a neutral backdrop to the spectacular view.

RKD ARCHITECTS

guastavino's

LOCATION: **NEW YORK, USA**
ARCHITECT/DESIGNER: **CONRAN & PARTNERS, LONDON, UK**

The Queensborough Bridge in New York was built at the end of the 19th century to allow traffic to flow across the East River and connect mid-town and Queens. Underneath the arches of the bridge on the Manhattan side, great vaults were constructed from white glazed terracotta tiles in a self-supporting technique pioneered by Gustav Eiffel. The effect is cathedral-like both in terms of the scale and linear sculptural form generated.

Outside, the plaza space has been designed as a pocket park, which is populated by benches, trees, planters and people. A new glazed pavilion building designed by Conran & Partners marks the entrance to the Conran Shop.

The pavilion is a showcase for the best in contemporary furniture and design. Located beneath the bridge, the space is characterised by the heroic concrete footings of the structure above. These were excavated to create the under-croft and the rough quality of the columns alludes to the archaeological nature of the space. Around these elements sit contemporary timber and zinc fixtures and fittings within an otherwise white modernist space.

The restaurant is understood as a series of components or mechanisms, which are floating within the body of the 'classical space'. A series of layers has been inserted working from front to back. The diner participates in the cinematic experience of seeing and being seen. The kitchen provides a dynamic backdrop to the operation and is arranged on two floors behind a second full height glass screen. At ground level, the bar occupies the entrance area and creates a gently glowing barrier between drinking, smoking and eating. The brasserie is situated beneath the underbelly of the deck; a curved timber skin is stretched over a skeleton containing servicing. The mezzanine has a cocktail lounge and upper deck dining floating above the more informal brasserie.

ica bar

LOCATION: **LONDON, UK**
ARCHITECT/DESIGNER: **GRAEME WILLIAMSON AND ZOË SMITH, BLOCK ARCHITECTURE, LONDON, UK**

The bar at the ICA was completed in 1999 for a budget of around £75,000. Essentially, the ICA explores the relationship between the borrowed and the made through the use of materials out of their expected contexts. The brief for this project was to create an environment that was flexible in use, particularly between day and night, and would be accessible to a varied clientele. The architects aimed to create a space which uses recognisable elements to generate this accessibility.

The site was defined as the intersection of art gallery, book shop, cinema, theatre, conference room and media centre, to create a place where people could meet, hold small events i.e. talks, book-readings, launches, and also host evening events such as club or DJ nights. The design programme had to address all these different functions.

The intention was to give the bar a sense of its own identity within the institute and for it to act as respite/oasis from the gallery spaces. This distinction was achieved through the use of perhaps unexpected materials such as Cellbond (normally employed in aircraft construction) and white fireclay urinal slabs from Armitage Shanks. The incorporation of such familiar materials was deliberate, although they were reconfigured in an unexpected context.

The back bar is made up of exposed edge plywood strip which was custom made as a panel material This is used again as the table tops; the form of the tables was cut and laminated together to produce a solid surface.

The lighting is directional and can be dimmed to create a variable ambience.

Seating is on special edition, translucent polyprop chairs with unfinished steel work. These chairs were also chosen for their familiarity. The polyprop is the most utilitarian of any chair, a fact accentuated by stripping it back to illustrate its constituent materials.

GRAEME WILLIAMSON AND ZOË SMITH, BLOCK ARCHITECTURE

GRAEME WILLIAMSON AND ZOË SMITH, BLOCK ARCHITECTURE

ICA BAR

isola

LOCATION: **LONDON, UK**
ARCHITECT/DESIGNER: **ANDY MARTIN ASSOCIATES, LONDON, UK**

Following the creation of the hugely successful Mash restaurants, Andy Martin Associates have completed Oliver Peyton's largest project to date, Isola restaurant.

Andy's concept for Isola is a marked departure from his former highly stylised designs; his latest project's emphasis is concentrated upon simplicity and sensitivity, an indulgence of the senses. Situated between Scotch House and Mr Chow's, the £4 million Italian restaurant has a 25 metre long dominating glass front, which casts an imposing reflection upon its surrounding Knightsbridge counterparts. Isola consists of two dining areas, the upper level dedicated to fine dining and the lower level to brasserie style eating.

Andy Martin Associates have retained the original internal form of the building into which has been inserted an 'L' shape form that is seen floating within these designated spatial confines. This weightless configuration (*isola* in Italian means island) creates the upper level of the restaurant and appears to hover above street level.

Contrasting materials have been used to define the relative spaces – each being pushed to its limit with the objective of producing 3D space from a 2D surface. Upon entering Isola, the guest is enveloped by highly reflective stainless steel. Cantilevered stairs and concrete rendering link and flow between dining levels. Timber parquet is laid in a graphic Escher pattern; it clings to the ceiling in the brasserie, wrapping itself around the island, continuing on to the floor and dominant wall of the upper level. Lower level flooring is in a cooler gridded agglomerate marble. These materials contrast and complement, developing their own personalities.

Andy Martin Associates were commissioned to create Isola in its entirety – furniture, lights, and objects; these designs work in partnership with the interior to define and sculpt the space. On the ground floor, Italian sports car manufacturers Ferrari upholstered the floating leather clad booths that are equipped with individual lighting systems to create an atmosphere of semi private dining. Venini were commissioned to produce glass elements for the six chandeliers that complete the space. The lower level, with its leather-clad sofa-style chairs, simulates an almost domestic eating environment – guests can share large plates of pasta or fish. Isola is completely stripped of styles, ideals and forms. The main concern was to find the essence of architecture – to convey the way things feel, to stimulate touch and smell and discover how material reality is perceived. The architecture of Isola is conceived as a timeless capsule, a sensitive container for enjoying the perfect meal.

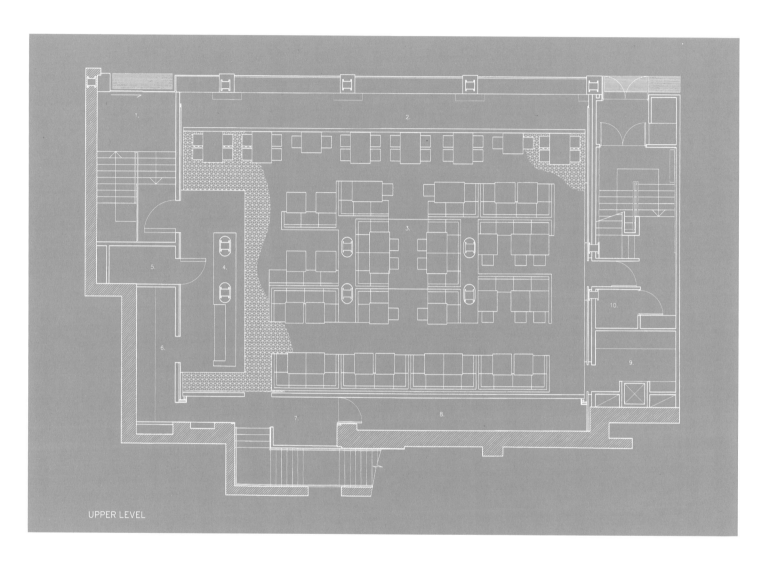

UPPER LEVEL

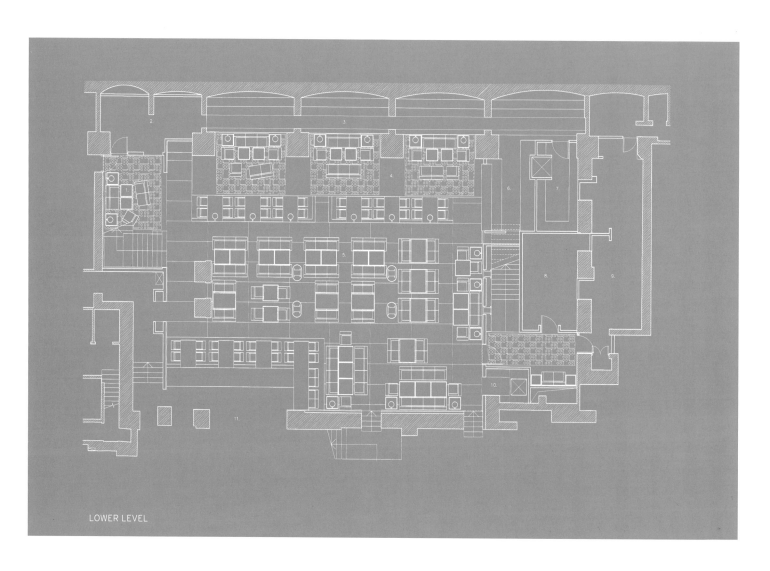

LOWER LEVEL

ANDY MARTIN ASSOCIATES

izakaya koi

LOCATION: MALMÖ, SWEDEN
ARCHITECT/DESIGNER: JONAS LINDVALL/VERTIGO ARKITEKTUR & DESIGN, MALMÖ, SWEDEN

The project was to design a Japanese sushi bar/restaurant.
The restaurant is situated in the old part of Malmö, in southern
Sweden, in a building that dates back to 1750. The room that
is the actual restaurant is roughly 70 square metres.

The clients wanted a restaurant with both a bar and a
dining area as well as a sushi kitchen situated inside the bar.

One of the most important issues when designing this
space was to answer the question: How do the people who are
going to occupy these spaces want to feel? The architects made
the observation that particularly when entering a restaurant
for the first time, the guest may experience a sense of
desertion - of being left to their own devices among strangers.
To combat this sense of isolation, the architects strove to
provide the guests with a chance to anchor themselves in
their new environment, to feel comfortable immediately after
entering the space.

To achieve a sense of rhythm, the programme sought
to create two different characters within the room. The ceiling
was lowered to create a greater feeling of intimacy in the bar
section with sparkling, directed halogen lights. This is in direct
contrast to the dining area which has more diffuse, suspended
lamps with normal lightbulbs.

The materials and forms employed were intended to
provide no more than a subtle hint into what is Japanese,
rather than operating to effect what could well be regarded
as a cliché. To this end, the project was given a strong graphic
quality. Working with white oiled ash, light green/yellow walls,
a hue that can be found in the glazing on traditional Japanese
ceramics and the shape of barstool seats derived from Asian
roof ridges were some of the means used to bring a serene
Japanese feel to the space. Proportions and dimensions
and the chain of measurements were also pointed to enhance
this feeling.

The dominant idea was to create a simple space that would
give people the possibility of enjoying their food in a venue
ideally suited to the purpose.

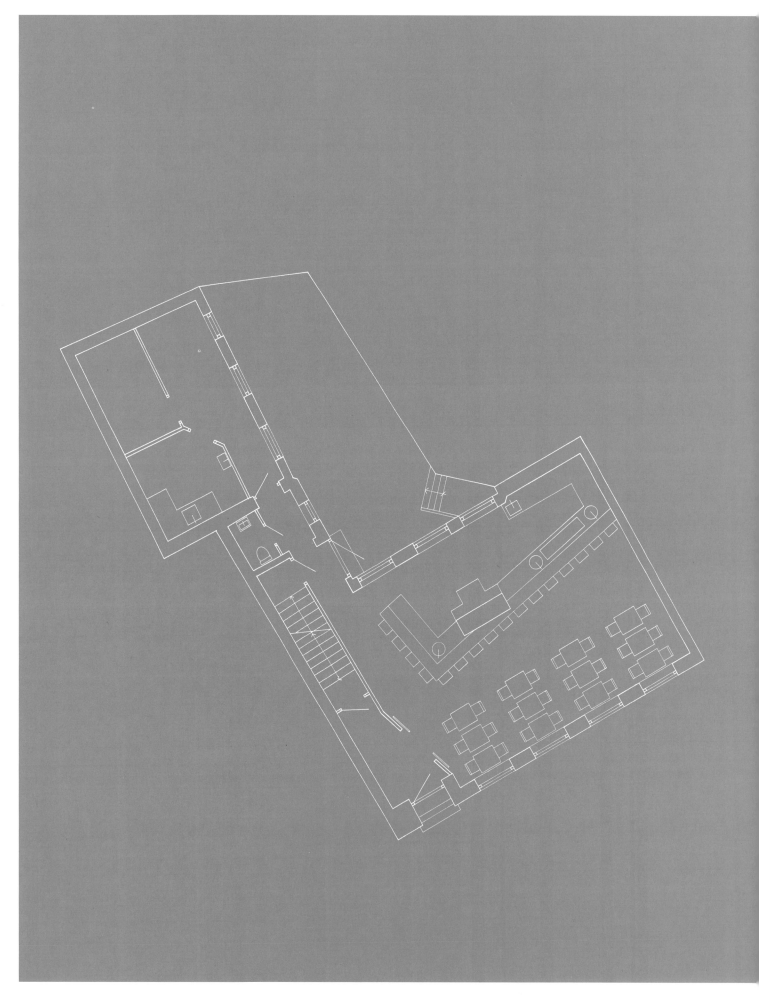

JONAS LINDVALL/VERTIGO ARKITEKTUR & DESIGN

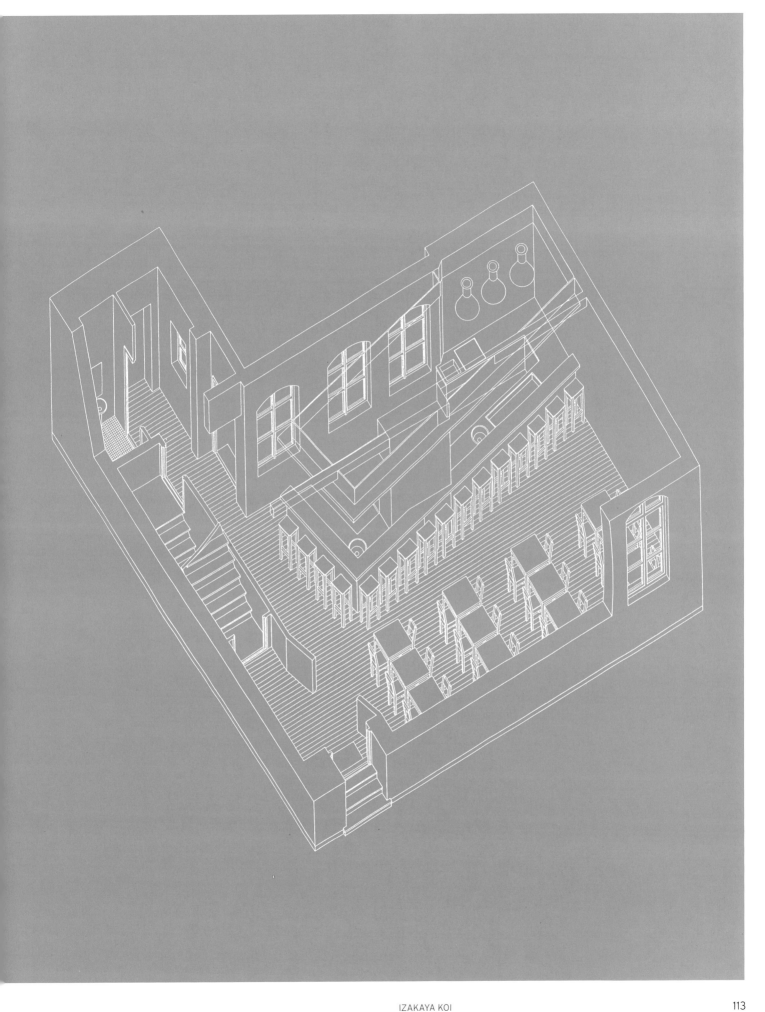

JONAS LINDVALL/VERTIGO ARKITEKTUR & DESIGN

the light

LOCATION: **LONDON, UK**
ARCHITECT/DESIGNER: **WAUGH THISTLETON, LONDON, UK**

As the first building encountered from the City, The Light forms a fitting and prestigious entrance to the London Borough of Hackney. As London's first and only remaining purpose built electricity power station, it played a key role in the development of electricity generation worldwide. This stunning and historically important building was rescued from near collapse in August 1999 and transformed into a popular restaurant and bar.

The brick fabric of the entire building was extensively cleaned both inside and out and the exterior stonework was restored. Where elements of the building had been lost, such as entrance doors and a section of the roof, new elements were introduced. Rather than attempt to mimic the original building and guess at the form of these elements, they were rebuilt in a contemporary fashion to complement the original.

In approaching the new reconstruction, Waugh Thistleton were concerned that the qualities and detail of the original building should not be overwhelmed by the new. Equally it was important that the interventions should be bold and expressive of the current purpose.

WAUGH THISTLETON

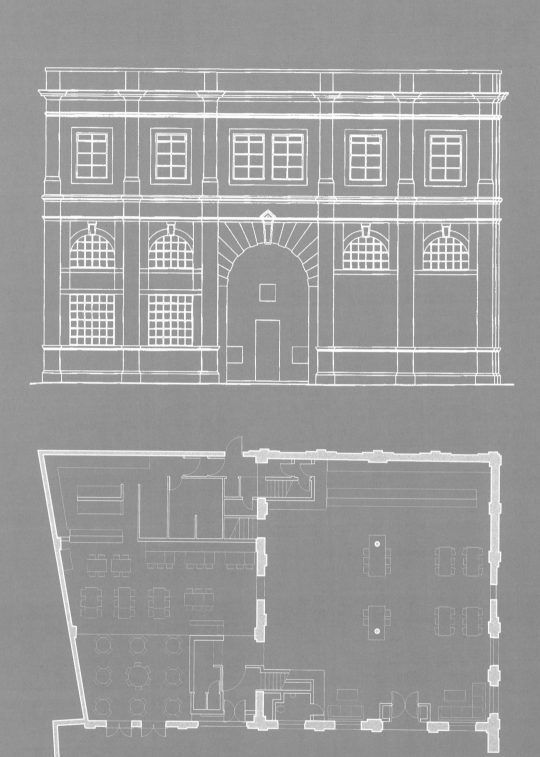

GROUND FLOOR

WAUGH THISTLETON

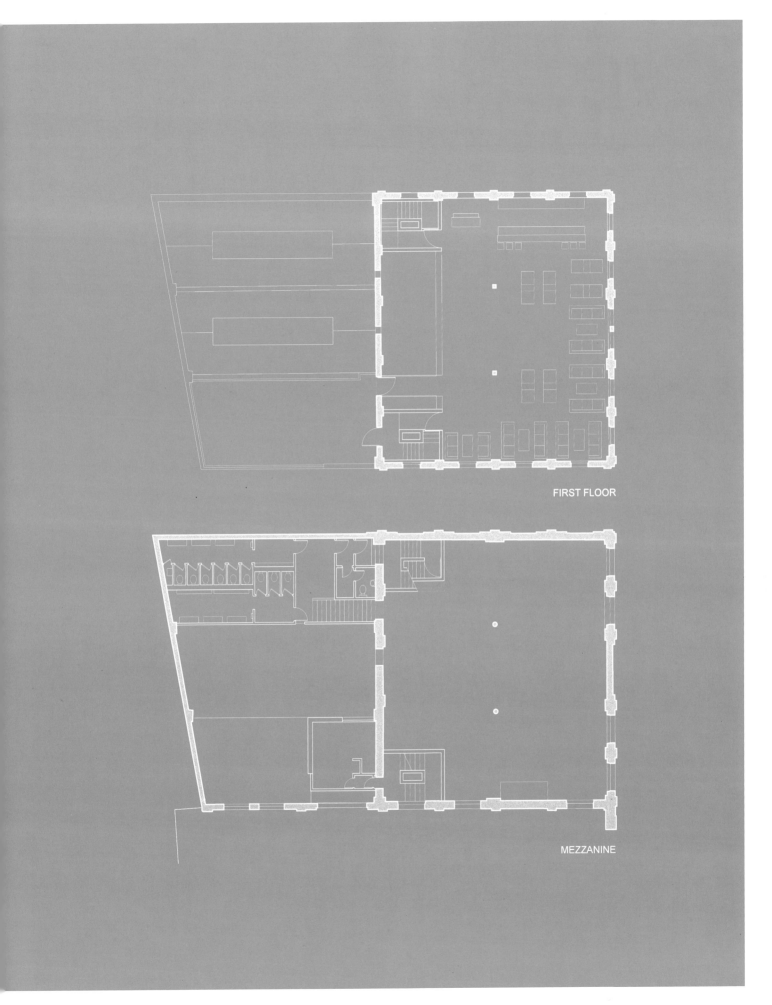

FIRST FLOOR

MEZZANINE

love

LOCATION: **OXFORD, UK**
ARCHITECT/DESIGNER: **PAUL DALY DESIGN STUDIO, LONDON, UK**

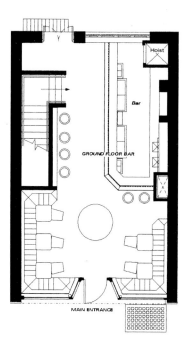

Love's compact space has been designed as a vibrant, style-conscious, crowd pulling backdrop for clubbing in the heart of Oxford.

The construction is reminiscent of *Dr Who*'s Tardis: the ground floor area is contained in one building while the basement extends over two. This almost sci-fi effect is enhanced by the impact of the glass floor on to which people step immediately they enter the venue – sharp and innovative, providing a view of the basement below it anticipates the excitement of the dance floor and of its more intimate spaces. With its palette of red, green and gold the programme successfully combines the sexual invitation of the bordello with the thrill of Kubrick's *2001*.

A circular bulkhead above the glass floor mimics the glass cut out and houses pin spots which penetrate the opening to the basement below. The staircase to the basement is made from wood and metal leading to a concrete base, materials that set the basement's raw tone. Chinese slate adds depth and the echo it provides makes one aware of one's dancing feet. Under the street are small alcoves or 'love pods' intended as cosy, even intimate hideaways for individuals or small groups. The DJ stands in this VIP area and plays through the wall to the dance floor on the other side, the base speakers make up the stage for the dancers ...

PAUL DALY DESIGN STUDIO

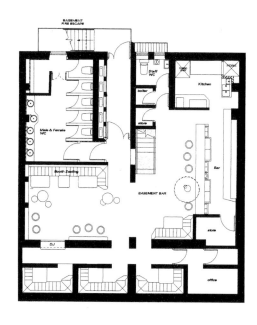

PAUL DALY DESIGN STUDIO

monto restaurant and brasserie

LOCATION: THESSALONIKI, GREECE
ARCHITECT/DESIGNER: BARR GAZETAS, LONDON, UK

Monto restaurant is situated in a new shopping complex just off the main shopping street in Thessaloniki, Greece. Although the centre is in a prominent position, the entrance to the restaurant is off a much quieter street with a very small street frontage. As the restaurant is hidden away it was important to use memorable design to create a striking destination and a reason to return. Since opening in 1999 this has proven to be the case; the restaurant is well known and the café has become a popular meeting place in the city.

The primary design decision was to make the entrance an event in itself. The client had already asked for the café and restaurant to be separated spaces so the idea was conceived that the kitchen could divide the spaces but supply both.

Curved plasterboard links through into the restaurant area. The opposite wall is clad in copper and leans into the space. Diagonal timber flooring acts as a contrast to the walls.

The restaurant area is mainly white space, which spills out into a hidden courtyard with glass block cladding.

To the right the café opens up into a contrasting space derived from a helix spiral at a four-degree slope. A curving sloping ramp of glass winds around a vertical feature, which is used as a disc jockey booth. Stools line the route and the copper wall reappears revealing the kitchen as a copper clad box within the organic spaces. A series of eating booths is formed within the space and again these are clad in copper.

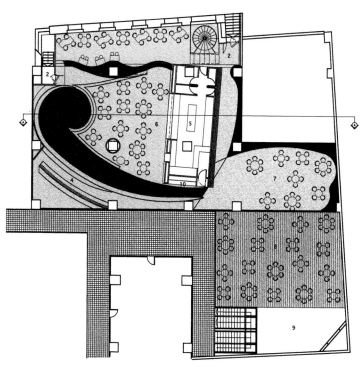

BARR GAZETAS

the morrison hotel

LOCATION: **DUBLIN, REPUBLIC OF IRELAND**
ARCHITECT/DESIGNER: **DOUGLAS | WALLACE, DUBLIN, REPUBLIC OF IRELAND**

As the architects and designers for The Morrison Hotel, Douglas | Wallace were commissioned to create bar and restaurant areas at the cutting edge of design to differentiate The Morrison from other hotels in Dublin.

The design of the interior space of the bars and restaurant uses the theme of East meets West, combining a rich mix of materials both dark and light.

The public can access the bars and restaurant through the vast riverside entrance on Dublin quay. A quiet side entrance leads to the hotel reception for guests. In order to link these two areas together and ensure they do not have the appearance of being separate entities, there is a yellow wall that runs from front to back and from the very top of the hotel to the bottom. This unifies not only the public areas with the hotel but also all the floors above.

On the ground floor there are two bars - The Morrison Bar on the left and The Café Bar on the right. While The Morrison Bar is both lit and designed as an evening location, the much larger Café Bar is an all day and all night location.

To cope with this continual trade, The Café Bar has the benefit of large window space on two sides. Everything is low level - tables, chairs, lighting and even backgammon boards. The lighting design is very successful in using natural daylight to illuminate the space, leading to a feeling of serenity in the evening. The overwhelming mood is one of spaciousness and rich design in the centre of a pulsating cosmopolitan city.

One of the strongest visual elements throughout is the use of ebonised American red oak, which can be found on every floor including in the public toilets. This is combined with Portuguese limestone and walls of polished armourcoat plaster, curtains of silk-velvet and deep-pile handmade carpets. The environment is softened by the touch of John Rocha, the hotel's creative consultant.

All the furniture used within the bars and restaurant was bespoke for The Morrison and complements both the modernity of the architecture and the richness of texture of the materials. Furniture was designed and made by Orior in Newry. Seating is varied and luxurious, ranging from two or three seater sofas, to leather box chairs to dining chairs upholstered in white fabric.

The effective display of contemporary art and sculpture is very prominent throughout the building. In the late-night Lobo Bar stands a 15-foot Africanesque head, sculpted from 600 cubic feet of 2 inch mahogany by Eoin Byrne. The artist Clea van der Grijn painted the giant tryptich featured in the Halo Restaurant.

A glass atrium descends into the Halo Restaurant from three storeys. The restaurant is washed over by ever changing light and shade which allows its fusion style cooking to be enjoyed in a dramatic architectural space.

The overriding quality of The Morrison is the attention to detail. The client has encouraged rather than stifled creativity with the result that Dublin now has a truly international destination hotel.

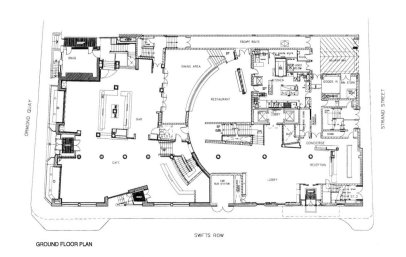

GROUND FLOOR PLAN

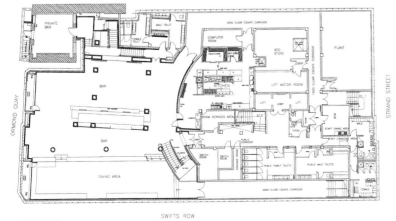

BASEMENT PLAN

mpv

LOCATION: **LEEDS, UK**
ARCHITECT/DESIGNER: **UNION NORTH, LIVERPOOL, UK**

The brief was to develop as a bar/club/pavement café a set of four railway arches to replace existing retail and light industrial units.

The project is situated at a significant distance from the main buzz of Assembly Street and was therefore conceived as a destination in its own right with a striking visual identity. The design constraints posed by the arches immediately suggested free standing units and this with the effective legal limit on the area of the first floor space generated the distinctive profile of the pods, fitting the arch closely at low level, then tapering inwards above to follow the reduction in floor area.

Union North's own enthusiasm for no fuss, ergonomically driven, integrated industrial design led to the arresting external image of the four glossy pods emerging from the cocooning arches. Internally the division into four units was organised to accommodate a diversity of functions and ambiences including chill out lounge, clubroom, cocktail bar and function rooms; there was potential space for live music, comedy and snack food service.

Once the pod design was finalised, other design elements fell naturally into place: existing Jack arches allow access between pods by articulated link corridors; the narrow leftover slot behind the viaduct becomes a connecting service void; and ventilation plant is suspended from the rear walls of the pods.

In the search for appropriate construction techniques and materials, budgetary constraints and the exposure of the shell to wear and tear pointed towards a Liverpool ship repair firm. In keeping with Union North's industrial aesthetic the pods were prefabricated in 2 metre segments, that dimension dictated by material and transportation retraints. Each segment was fully welded and painted in Liverpool before trucking to site for rapid assembly necessitated by Railtrack's restrictions for crane installation. Completed shells were then coated internally and sprayed with insulating foam.

As shells were completed, a conventional interior fit out followed. An enveloping wrap around aesthetic was sought to blur wall, floor and ceiling into a single unified membrane of lacquered fair faced plywood. All services were minimised or hidden. Flip up doors double as canopies and security doors.

A protected route from the upper floor areas direct to the exterior was required. This was articulated as a sculpted tube sweeping down through the ceiling and out through the glazed screen terminating in clam shell exit doors.

With the industrial aesthetic of the viaduct and Railtrack's operation complemented in the materials and futuristic design of the pods, this bar/club and pavement café articulates a bold, vibrant and human intervention in what was formerly an unimaginatively utilised urban commercial space.

UNION NORTH

oxo tower
restaurant

LOCATION: **LONDON, UK**
ARCHITECT/DESIGNER: **LIFSCHUTZ DAVIDSON, LONDON, UK**

The new eighth floor extension is the latest in a series of
alterations to a building originally constructed in 1890 to serve
as the Post Office's generating station. The building was
extended and converted in the 1920s to become a meat
warehouse and had the Oxo Tower, an eight storey high
concrete shell, added in the 1930s. The Oxo logo was cut
into the tower as fenestration to get around prohibitions
on advertising on the river front.

The restaurant is only one of many uses in the building;
also present are shops, designer maker workshops and low rent
housing. But the rooftop provided a special opportunity for
a spectacular structure that would cap the building and provide
rental income to subsidise the 78 co-op apartment units below.

The structure of the roof was designed to complement
rather than conflict with the Oxo Tower and provide stunning
views – hence the continuous wing shaped monopitch that
sweeps up to 5 metres above the floor in the elevation facing
the river.

Main circulation is via lifts in the core under the tower
leading to an eighth floor landing with a spectacular aspect
over south London. From here visitors can walk to the free
public viewing gallery on the riverside or enter either the
brasserie or restaurant to the east and west.

Within each of these spaces kitchens, toilets and other
services are grouped centrally to leave the perimeter free
for views. The soffit flows up to the dramatic glazed north wall,
which is made of frameless glazing, suspended from the roof –
an arrangement that eliminates structure on the lower part
of the facade. As a result views over the river are unimpeded,
with canted sliding doors giving access to an exterior terrace.

LIFSCHUTZ DAVIDSON

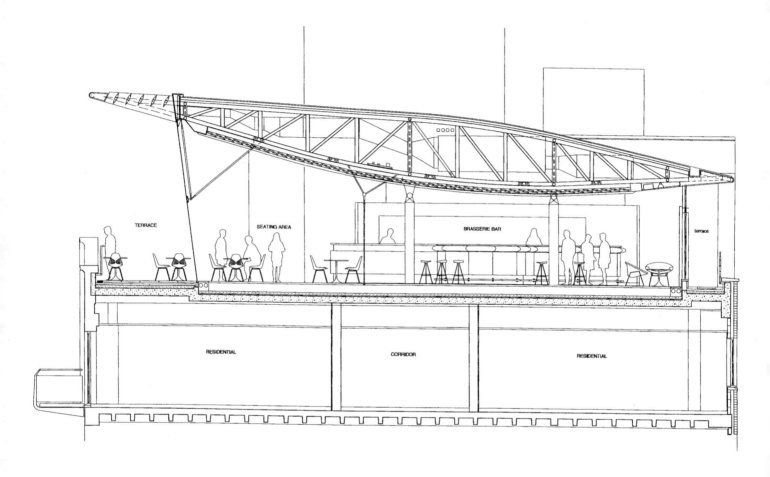

TERRACE SEATING AREA BRASSERIE BAR terrace

RESIDENTIAL CORRIDOR RESIDENTIAL

LIFSCHUTZ DAVIDSON

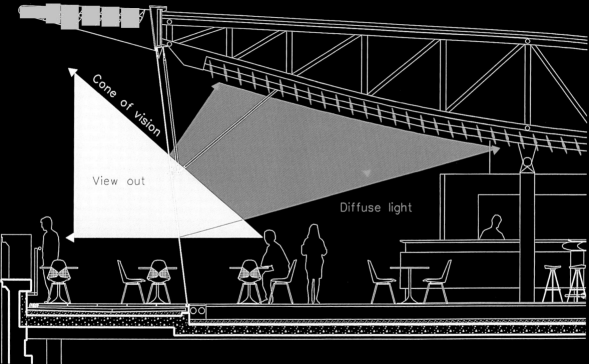

Cone of vision

View out

Diffuse light

pleven beer kiosk

LOCATION: **SOFIA, BULGARIA**
ARCHITECT/DESIGNER: **NOBLE ASSOCIATES, LONDON, UK**

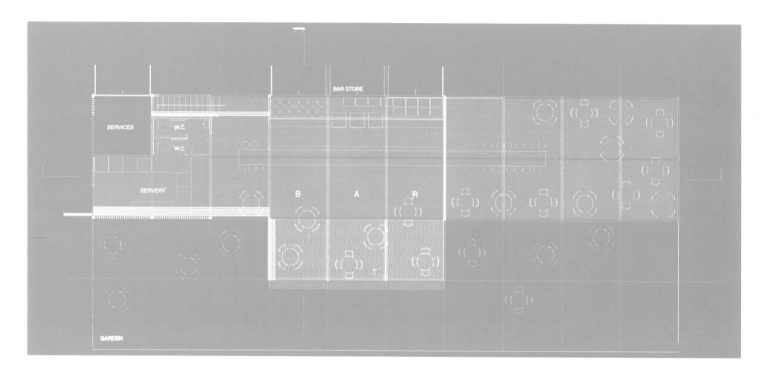

Noble Associates were approached by Pleven, a brewery in Bulgaria, to design a new idea 'kiosk' – a structure that can be re-erected in other locations or at other times. A 'portable' bar which could exist any place anywhere. The brief responds to the market in a country where the summers are very hot and people spend a great deal of time outside, where the beer companies hold beer festivals as a good way to establish or support a brand, launch a new product and get the public to buy beer.

This portable bar was a very simple and rational structure, neo-classical in its concept, and neo-Grecian in its lack of detail. A demountable set of parts, all built from timber, it was developed around the idea of a single panel that could be used for floors or walls, all slatted, either as brise-soleil or self-draining for the floor.

A tent structure was integrated to the design and it was built, in the main park in the middle of Sofia, in Bulgaria, with a draped tent structure off the front, all the framings and claddings in heavily knotted pine, including an all pine bar. It has proved a commercial success for Pleven during the last two summers.

the pool

LOCATION: **LONDON, UK**
ARCHITECT/DESIGNER: **FORSTER INC, LONDON, UK**

The design brief was to create a bar and restaurant with American pool tables, bars on two levels, a low seat lounge and a dance floor in London's fashionable Shoreditch.

The particular challenges with this project were to create a comfortable yet animated interior in which the mix of uses overlap.

To create a design which runs coherently through the ground floor to the basement whilst maintaining different atmospheres and uses on each floor.

To overcome the association of pool playing with seedy dives and create an atmosphere that would encourage women as well as men to play and to utilise an existing centrally located staircase.

Elements of particular design interest are the use of strong colours and rich textural materials inviting people to spend time and relax.

Materials include reclaimed teak, dark brown mosaic tiles and a deeply stained floor with a palette of greens and deep reds, individually designed high and low bar stools, dining chairs and tables, banquette seating and low tables specifically for the pool. The bar is exposed from the street through large windows with the central staircase leading under the bar to the basement bar and lounge.

Forster Incorporated's design approach has created an animated environment rich in texture and colours that combines function with innovative aesthetics.

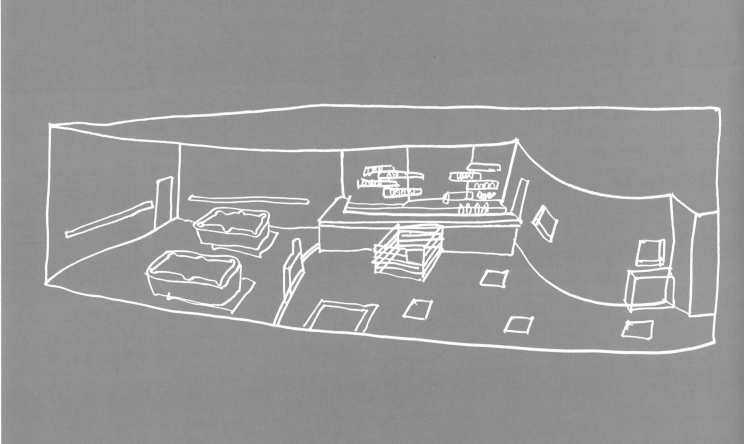

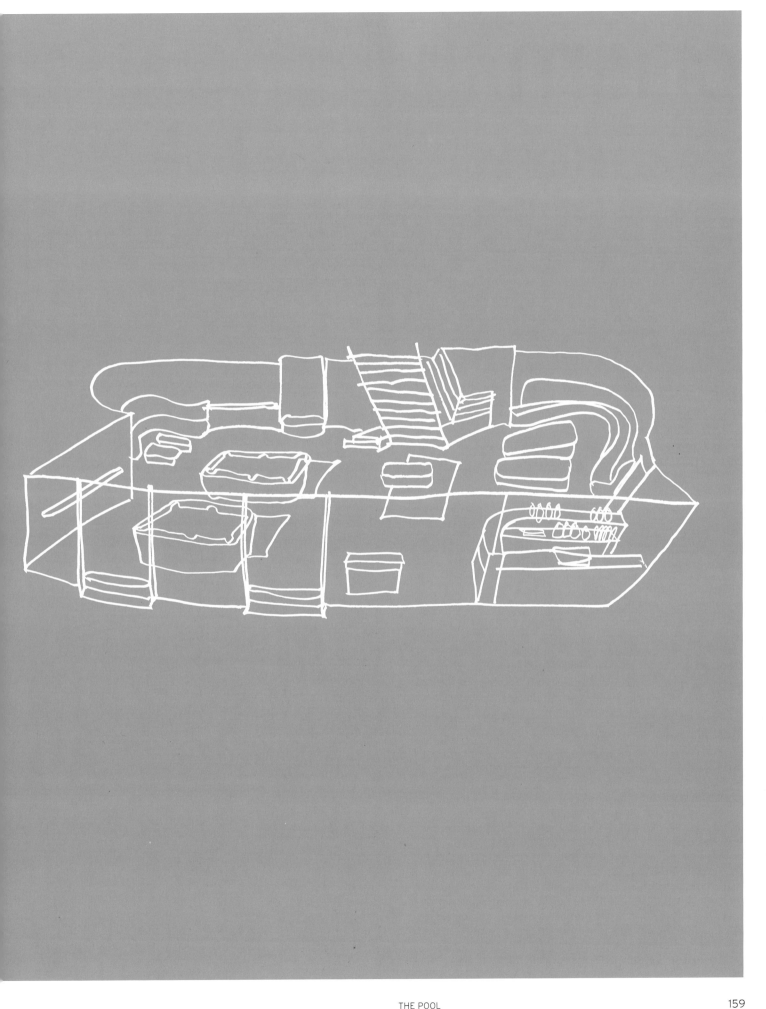

prism

LOCATION: **LONDON, UK**
ARCHITECT/DESIGNER: **LIFSCHUTZ DAVIDSON, LONDON, UK**

147 Leadenhall Street was formerly a bank constructed in 1927 and now listed Grade II. The building is situated opposite Lloyds Insurance Building in the heart of the City of London.

The restaurant is arranged over three levels - mezzanine, ground and basement - with most of the kitchens and service space at the lowest level.

The main restaurant is in the former banking hall, which has been carefully restored to its former condition - a magnificent double height space in which the bar and tables are placed in a calm and generous grid. Seating is in red leather Brno chairs by Mies van der Rohe; the bar is purpose designed in stainless steel mesh with a crushed glass countertop.

The exterior of this space is a newly enclosed light well, clad in light stone and carefully lit to enhance the little daylight that penetrates. This external 'orangery' is an essential outlet for the views from the main restaurant space, and contains seating and tables for snacks and drinks.

The basement bar is, by contrast, a cosy and intimate space, carefully detailed in tactile materials, including walnut and leather tones and textures, drawn from the palette used in luxury cars. A cream leather banquette runs along the full length of the space and conceals lighting and air-conditioning; the bar runs along the other wall.

Private dining rooms are provided at ground and mezzanine level, the latter with splendid views over the main restaurant.

The suspended ceiling is formed of rotating aerofoils that are painted dark blue on one face and white on the other. At night the darker surface is exposed and this works in combination with the sloping glass wall to minimise reflections - on the same principle as the parcel shelf reduces reflection from the glass face of the instrument panel of the car.

The white side of the aerofoil is exposed during the day to provide a lighter, more vibrant feel to the restaurant. The pitch of the louvres can be adjusted to minimise or maximise acoustic absorption. Lighting from behind the louvres accentuates the saturated blue colour at night/white during dull days. Furniture is generally purpose designed with tables and chairs chosen from 20th-century classics by Eames and Bertoia.

The restaurant and its viewing gallery attracts about 40,000 visitors and has been a major catalyst for regeneration within the area.

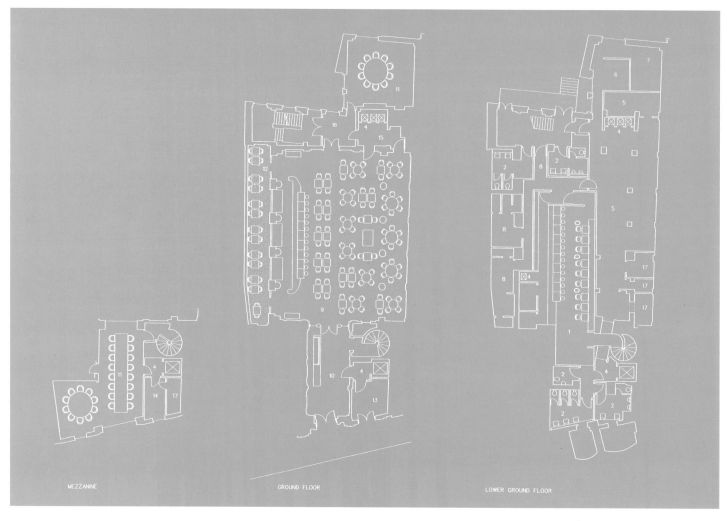

MEZZANINE

GROUND FLOOR

LOWER GROUND FLOOR

LIFSCHUTZ DAVIDSON

LIFSCHUTZ DAVIDSON

red room

LOCATION: SAN FRANCISCO
ARCHITECT/DESIGNER: FUN DISPLAY, SAN FRANCISCO, USA

Red Room, the description is in the name – red ceiling, red walls, red floor and red furniture. The 900 square foot bar adjacent to the Commodore Hotel at 827 Sutter Street, San Francisco is drenched completely in monochromatic red. Patrons enter through a portal whose walls are made of stacked bottles filled with red liquid. A giant red Martini glass filled with bubbling water sways mechanically back and forth above the back bar.

The initial inspiration behind the Red Room was a desire to create a kind of devilishly glamourous 'hell' bar. The design has been typified as 'a successful blend of glamour and kitsch'. Richly textured, sensuous fabrics, Italian glass mosaic tiles, hand carved columns and back-lit glass walls evoke images of a cosy Old Hollywood get-away, while the giant red Martini glass fountain and the house cosmopolitan style take you all the way to Las Vegas.

WWC

Storage

Gold
Room

MWC

FUN DISPLAY

ronnie scott's

LOCATION: **BIRMINGHAM, UK**
ARCHITECT/DESIGNER: **PATRICK CASEY, AVALON DESIGN GROUP, BIRMINGHAM, UK**

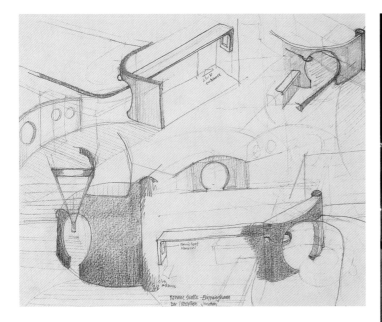

The mystical scent of incense hangs heavy in the air and greets you when first entering the Front Room at Ronnie Scott's. A heady palette of gold, bronze and copper, oriental red and Manhattan blue with splashes of purple and green combines to provide a visual feast. The juxtaposition of tactile textures and surfaces from rough-cast plaster to smooth blue walls, leather and velvet, timber to carpet, cactus and lilies and the play of light and shade create an ambience of sensuality, opulence and luxury.

Shape and form play a role in defining this space; most pronounced, the curved wall travelling outside to inside that introduces another curved wall with circular entrance highlighted in gold. This announces the entrance and journey through the corridor to the club room which are linked by a sleek streamlined ceiling enhanced by a faint purple glow of light. Metaphorical symbols, paintings and sculptures by local artists combined with an eclectic design and strong ethnic mix, reflect Birmingham's multicultural diversity.

Away from and yet within the hustle and bustle of Broad Street (Birmingham's answer to Leicester Square), the Front Room at Ronnie Scott's provides an oasis of calm, a feeling of a spiritual moment that envelopes, caresses and soothes. This is fantasy realised.

PATRICK CASEY, AVALON DESIGN GROUP

ruby foo's

LOCATION: **NEW YORK, USA**
ARCHITECT/DESIGNER: **ROCKWELL GROUP, NEW YORK, USA**

In collaboration with Steve Hanson, Rockwell Group has transformed this 10,000 foot space into a comfortable warm environment, fashioning the Ruby Foo's Dim Sum and Sushi Palace as a playful and handsome reinterpretation of Old Mott Street food emporiums. The result is a bright inventive tribute to the many Asian influences that have helped to shape western culinary and cultural experience.

Just as the menu spans the Far East, so does the restaurant design. A fabulous two-level interior incorporates both subtle and vibrant elements of Asian life. For example, the big bold calligraphic characters are abstracted from the context of China Town's neon signs and used to adorn the restaurant's brightly coloured tabletops. A dramatic free standing staircase curves upwards in front of the 30 foot high red lacquered wall resembling a giant bento box. Its larger than life compartments display everyday Asian objects such as painted fans, ceramic bowls, chopsticks and bamboo steamers, as well as unique items including a bronze gong, velvet slippers, huge vases and an antique Buddha.

Rockwell group has also created an impressive duplex sushi bar with white walls that glow like Chinese lanterns – literally a two-storey stage of action and rhythm. The sushi bar becomes the focal point of each floor of the restaurant. Finally, hundreds of shiny colourful mahjong tiles are cleverly transformed into a graceful playful mosaic screen separating the roomy bar area from the dramatic staircase.

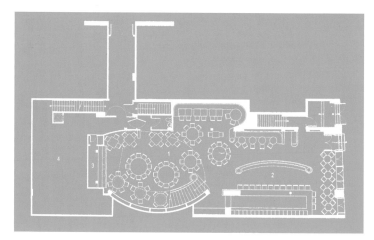

severnshed restaurant

LOCATION: **BRISTOL, UK**
ARCHITECT/DESIGNER: **PETER MEACOCK/CENTRAL WORKSHOP, BRISTOL, UK**

Peter Meacock's approach was to retain the essential characteristics of the original design and modify the building elements to achieve a fully integrated and comfortable environment for the enjoyment of both customers and staff. He calls his approach 'functional reductivism', whereby each element is analysed to achieve its most flexible and efficient form and essential quality. Explicitly, this approach is not minimalist. Use and fitness for purpose are paramount, also the essential integrity of materials and surface. Less is more – more is less. Aesthetic concerns do not override functional requirements.

Externally the building has been carefully repaired to retain its integrity as a boat shed adjacent to the docks. The shed's full height sliding doors are pulled back each day to reveal a secondary set of timber glazed doors within, forming the weather seal. The free spanning interior space has been modified to retain the spirit of the original building, its spatial qualities and its former uses. The wall surfaces are broken up to frame the original cast iron columns. A drink shelf is inserted at a comfortable height to allow people to look out at the periphery of the building. The walls do not meet the roof and a strip of continuous glazing allows fragmented light to bounce off the river to emblazon the roof timbers with undulating light. The seating layout is both egalitarian and formal. Rows of tables and chairs in the restaurant and bar are exactly the same, only the service distinguishes the two areas.

The centrepiece, a stainless steel Hoverbar, defines the restaurant and bar areas. The Hoverbar is conceived as a freestanding sculptural object of 5 tons, which operates as a fully functioning piece of commercial equipment that contains an espresso machine, freezers, refrigerators, sinks and glass washer. It separates the bar/café and restaurant areas allowing a spatial flexibility unprecedented within the trade. For example, for a live music performance or function, the bar is simply moved to either end of the building creating a single large space, or if required a smaller more intimate area.

The bar is moved by connecting a compressed airline to inflate the four hover pads. It then rises by 18 millimetres to be pushed into position over the polished Dorset shingle concrete floor. All services are connected to the bar from a cast concrete trench that also acts as the duct for the air management system. To the bar/café side there is a continuous cherry wood bar surface of 7.2 metres set at a continental height of 1140 millimetres with bar stools along its length. Views between the restaurant and bar are maintained through a 6 metre by 900 millimetre continuous opening in the bar structure.

An in situ cast concrete balcony cantilevers 3 metres over the water offering south-facing, outdoor seating with stunning views over the Floating Harbour to St Mary Redcliffe and Phoenix Wharf. It is covered by a continuous retractable awning with 'Paris' gas burners, extending the limits of al-fresco dining beyond the normal restrictions of the British weather.

The building has been designed as a music and art venue in addition to the restaurant operation with a sophisticated acoustics system incorporated to reduce sound levels to the outside of the building. Performances take place weekly with larger concerts each month, when the whole building is given over to the event. Art is continuously displayed, the ample wall space and external areas of Severnshed hosting the changing exhibitions.

A great deal of time was taken with the chef, Raviv Hadad, to design an easy to use kitchen. This is connected to the restaurant via a serving hatch to allow a view without distracting the cooks or the guests. Severnshed operates an organic kitchen including much organic meat and wild fish, with its wood burning oven producing regularly changing menus for both formal and café dining.

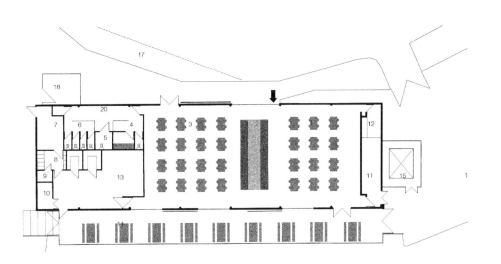

PETER MEACOCK/CENTRAL WORKSHOP

the sun & doves

LOCATION: **LONDON, UK**
ARCHITECT/DESIGNER: **FORSTER INC, LONDON, UK**

The new Sun and Doves took over an existing bar/restaurant site, a large, bare white space spanned by a cast concrete 'waffle' ceiling.

This space was divided using mid-height teak screens and booths and rows of banquette seating to create a series of more comfortable intimate spaces within the larger space.

Interior design is drawn from a rich palette of heather colours: dark brown, greys and lilacs mixed with upholstery sage, olive and deep burgundy. A pixilated image mural runs down one wall with the grid theme continued by the painted panels on the walls.

Additional lighting was introduced in the form of back lit acrylic panels which spill light across the bar with recessed and concealed strip lighting from behind and beneath the banquettes. An illuminated 'deli-strip' features a mixture of art objects and products available from the bar.

All the seating and screens are demountable and can be moved to create alternative layouts.

LOUNGE BAR
GALLERY & GRILL
TABLE & COUNTER SERVICE

COCKTAILS
CHAMPAGNES & WINES
BY THE GLASS

GRILL MENU
FULL MEALS & SNACKS
OYSTERS
APERITIVES & DIGESTIVES
ORANGE, DRAUGHT & BOTTLED BEERS
JUICES, SHAKES & MINERALS

VISUAL ARTS
PERFORMANCE & INSTALLATION
PRIVATE HIRE PARTIES & CATERING

COFFEES TEAS
CHOCOLATE & INFUSIONS

tatu bar + grill

LOCATION: BELFAST, NORTHERN IRELAND
ARCHITECT/DESIGNER: COLIN CONN, BOX ARCHITECTS, BELFAST, NORTHERN IRELAND

The bar and grill's front elevation on to the Lisburn Road is made up of a large projecting zinc canopy, the leading edge of the walnut cloud which hovers at high level over the timber decked external drinking area. This projection is most effective at night as powerful lights in the decking beam upwards bouncing off the underside of the silvery/grey zinc. The glass front to the building is masked in part by a large iroko screen which contains the signage and complements the transparency of the curtain wall.

The entrance porch is a zinc box punched through the glass wall which articulates the front facade. In the front bar, a 9 metre high space, the ceiling resembles a dark, heavy cloud – dark walnut with a 1 metre light slot around its perimeter giving a gravity defying impression. To one side, the dark walnut panelled wall is perforated by ventilation slots and punctuated by stainless steel and sandblasted lighting that has been custom designed. Walnut and alcantara benches and tables are situated directly under adjacent lighting. Glazing inserted in the perimeter slot in the ceiling allows light to trickle down the walnut wall.

The other side of this space is dominated by a 21 metre long in-situ concrete bar, which begins at the front door and runs into the rear lower bar area, stitching the two spaces together. Behind the bar a backlit wall provides an effective backdrop to the many coloured spirit bottles standing on display; below them, a glass and stainless steel lightbox further scatters coloured light up, through and beyond.

Ventilation is above the opening carved out for the bar service area; 20 'hairdryer' adjustable nozzles blow conditioned air towards people at the bar. Air is then extracted through slots in the plenum walnut wall.

The end wall of this space is directly opposite the entrance and is covered in protruding stainless steel pegs. The texture of this wall changes constantly as natural light from the edge of the walnut 'cloud' changes direction throughout the day, casting varying shadows from the stainless steel pegs. At night artificial light takes over – the roof is covered in spotlights directing light down the perimeter roof slot. This has an even more arresting effect on the end textured wall.

Under the textured end wall the rear area drops down into a much lower space. Here the rear wall has been removed and replaced with one of translucent glass which allows natural light to pour in during the day and is replaced by external lighting at night. This lower area is made up of two insertions into the existing raw concrete structure.

The VIP area is a raised walnut 'scoop' with a front drinking bar at which one can stand or sit, depending which side one is on. This bar is punctuated by specially designed lighting along its length.

The restaurant area is defined by a curved alcantara wall. It is furnished with cream carpets, leather sofas, standard lamps and walnut tables with integral lighting to convey a relaxed atmosphere.

The highly innovative washrooms continue the use of walnut and sandblasted glass with a communal handbasin in a walnut box located between toilet areas, allowing the hands of the opposite sex to be revealed, and also secret conversations...

COLIN CONN, BOX ARCHITECTS

COLIN CONN, BOX ARCHITECTS

COLIN CONN, BOX ARCHITECTS

taxim nightpark

LOCATION: **ISTANBUL, TURKEY**
ARCHITECT/DESIGNER: **BRANSON COATES ARCHITECTURE, LONDON, UK**

Taxim, a large and complex refurbishment, opened on New Year's Eve 1990. From the outset, the Turkish client Metin Fadillioglu wanted the place to have the feel of a nightpark, with a smart restaurant and a couple of dance spaces, including the massive discotheque. It is designed as a space intent on creating and reflecting movement, complemented by the layered walkways that dramatise the entrance, and the international signs of airports alongside traditional Turkish quotes.

The original building, an old dye works, is presented as a found object - a Duchampian reinterpretation of the commonplace. Evidence of the original shell is maintained throughout, with its peeling paint and projecting reinforcing rods. Retaining the old facade, the new windows were set well back from the outer columns producing the effect of a new building inside the old. The glass is sandblasted with a Turkish textile pattern that provides a traditional foothold to the vocabulary of the place, albeit at an unexpected scale. Inside, walls and floors have been selectively stripped out to make a series of spaces that slip into each other. As well as using a fine art method of staging throughout, three major works or art were commissioned. These include Mark Prizeman's vertical scroll painting in the entrance and Stuart Helm's wall paintings in the Sofa Room upstairs.

The restaurant is conceived as an elegant storey-bazaar, with tiled arches and layers of brightly dyed canvas softening the hardness of the factory building behind. It features elements like the longest-leather-sofa-in-the-world and the longest-bead-curtain-in-the-world. The latter, situated behind the bar, took four women three weeks to make, threading Turkish eye beads on to cables to make huge eye patterns. An elevated walkway links the restaurant to the discotheque, its route cutting across the entrance hall. It's simultaneously a people mover and a stage behind the bead curtain.

Downstairs the disco is interpreted as an airport runway studded with runway lights and markings. Aircraft luggage containers from Turkish Airlines make intimate video viewing booths. The airline also donated a scissors lift, on which the computerised lighting console is mounted. This lighting is mysterious rather than cathartic. Video projectors that turn to skim their images slowly across the old factory walls achieve a gentle wash of movement over the main dance floor. On the stage a painting by Nigel Coates integrates the airport and the city with the club. On one of those tri-wonder revolving hoardings, its forms and colours are perpetually shifting.

zinc bar & grill

LOCATION: **MANCHESTER, UK**
ARCHITECT/DESIGNER: **CONRAN & PARTNERS, LONDON, UK**

The site chosen for the first Zinc Bar & Grill outside London is the old Manchester Corn Exchange. Renamed the Triangle, this new development in the heart of Manchester's new Millennium Quarter houses three floors of contemporary retail and restaurant units.

The Zinc Bar & Grill design concept is a dynamic fusion of traditional French brasserie and contemporary dining. Here, the use of a few lavish elements is contrasted with a subtle, restrained background to create an arresting yet welcoming atmosphere. An initial juxtaposition of everyday with crafted elements provided a theme that developed into an aesthetic based on the unusual use of familiar finishes. Utilitarian materials such as concrete pavers, external textured render, rough sawn roofing battens, incandescent light bulbs and laminated timber veneer are carefully combined to create a simple modern restaurant interior.

The 140-seat restaurant is divided in two, the lower area at street level and the upper one level with the mall. A frameless glass balustrade, allowing maximum views from one space to the other separates the two levels. The timber-slatted ceiling is a strong element within the restaurant, running at a continuous height over both spaces to create a lofty bar area and a more intimate upper dining area.

The focal point of the lower area is the 6 metre long Zinc Bar intended to host the lively Manchester night scene. The dramatic back bar extends up to the 3.8 metre high ceiling, with stainless steel and glass shelving for the display of liquor bottles. Mirror panels at low level give glimpsed reflections of the street outside while clear glass panels at high level allow views through to the kitchen beyond. In the evening coloured lighting illuminates the bottles and spotlights cast shadows of the suspended glasses onto the bar floor, creating an area of vibrancy.

The upper level has as its focal point the open kitchen where diners can watch the preparation of their food. The stainless steel server counters are clad in white brick tiles and have a row of suspended Edison lamps over the top pass shelf. The dining space is in muted colours, with a natural timber slatted ceiling, concrete paved floor and pale MDF panelled walls. The natural oak tables and zinc-wrapped waiter stations have all been specially designed to complement the subtle but sensual palette.

Zinc Bar & Grill Manchester is conceived as a blueprint for future Zinc projects. Simple modular elements have been designed to be applied to a number of locations in a flexible manner to create individual but similar spaces. The location and character of each building will inform the combination of component parts to create an interior specific to its place. Through design simplicity and creative buying strategies, the aim is to create good value contemporary Zinc restaurant venues in all the UK's major cities.

LISTINGS

astro bar
AUSTURSTRAETI 22
REYKJAVIK ICELAND
T +354 552 9222

aureole
MANDALAY BAY
3799 LAS VEGAS BOULEVARD SOUTH
LAS VEGAS NV 89109 USA
T +1 702 632 7401

babe ruth's
255 FINCHLEY ROAD
LONDON NW3 6LU UK
T +44 (0)20 7433 3388

backflip
601 EDDY STREET
SAN FRANCISCO
CA 94109 USA
T +1 415 771 3547

bargo
80 ALBION STREET
GLASGOW G1 1NY UK
T +44 (0)141 553 4771

bierodrome
173-174 UPPER STREET
ISLINGTON
LONDON N1 1RG UK
T +44 (0)20 7226 5835

circus
1 UPPER JAMES STREET
SOHO
LONDON W1F 9DF UK
T +44 (0)20 7534 4000

le cirque 2000
455 MADISON AVENUE
NEW YORK NY 10022 USA
T +1 212 303 7788

the elbow room
64 CALL LANE
LEEDS LS1 6DT UK
T +44 (0)113 245 7011
WWW.ELBOW-ROOM.CO.UK

eyre brothers
70 LEONARD STREET
LONDON EC2A 4QX UK
T +44 (0)20 7613 5346

georges
CENTRE POMPIDOU
PLACE GEORGES POMPIDOU
19 RUE BEAUBOURG
75004 PARIS FRANCE
T +33 1 44 78 47 99

grand central
93 GREAT EASTERN STREET
LONDON EC2A 3HZ UK
T +44 (0)20 7613 4228

gravity bar
GUINNESS STOREHOUSE
ST JAMES' GATE DUBLIN 8
REPUBLIC OF IRELAND
T +353 (0)1 408 4800
WWW.GUINNESS-STOREHOUSE.COM

guastavino's
409 E 59TH STREET
NEW YORK NY 10022 USA
T +1 212 980 2455
WWW.GUASTAVINOS.COM

ica bar
THE MALL
LONDON SW1Y 5AH UK
T +44 (0)20 7930 3647
WWW.ICA.ORG.UK

isola
145 KNIGHTSBRIDGE
LONDON SW1X 7PA UK
T +44 (0)20 7838 1044

izakaya koi
LILLA TORG 5
211 34 MALMÖ SWEDEN
T +46 (0)40 757 00
WWW.KOI.SE

the light
233 SHOREDITCH STREET
LONDON E1 6PJ UK
T +44 (0)20 7247 8989

love
3 KING EDWARD STREET
OXFORD UK
T +44 (0)1865 200 011

monto restaurant and brasserie
PLATIA CENTRE
THESSALONIKI GREECE
T +00 30 310 554652

the morrison hotel
ORMOND QUAY
DUBLIN 1
REPUBLIC OF IRELAND
T +353 1 887 2400
WWW.MORRISONHOTEL.IE

mpv
5-8 CHURCH WALK
LEEDS LS2 7DP UK
T +44 (0)113 243 9486

oxo tower restaurant
RIVERSIDE
OXO TOWER WHARF
BARGE HOUSE STREET
LONDON SE1 9PH UK
T +44 (0)20 7803 3888
WWW.OXOTOWER.CO.UK

pleven beer kiosk
NO PERMANENT ADDRESS:
THIS IS A TEMPORARY STRUCTURE
ERECTED FROM TIME TO TIME BY
PLEVEN IN SOFIA, BULGARIA.

prism
147 LEADENHALL STREET
LONDON EC3V 4QT UK
T +44 (0)20 7256 3888

red room
827 SUTTER STREET
SAN FRANCISCO CA 94102 USA
T +1 415 346 7666

ronnie scott's
BROAD STREET
BIRMINGHAM B1 2HF UK
T +44 (0)121 643 4525

ruby foo's
2182 BROADWAY
NEW YORK
NY 10024-6612 USA
T +1 212 724 6700

severnshed restaurant
THE GROVE
HARBOURSIDE
BRISTOL BS1 4RB UK
T +44 (0)117 925 1212
WWW.SEVERNSHED.CO.UK

the sun and doves
80-82 UPPER STREET
ISLINGTON
LONDON N1 0NU UK
T +44 (0)20 7226 6500

tatu bar + grill
701 LISBURN ROAD
BELFAST BT9 7GU
NORTHERN IRELAND
T +44 (0)28 9038 0818
WWW.TA-TU.COM

zinc bar & grill
THE TRIANGLE
HANGING DITCH
MANCHESTER M4 3ES UK
T +44 (0)161 827 4200